BAY AREA BIKING

BAY AREA
BIKING

60 of the Best Road and Trail Rides

FIRST EDITION

Ann Marie Brown

AVALON
TRAVEL

FOGHORN OUTDOORS
BAY AREA BIKING
60 of the Best Road and Trail Rides

First Edition

Ann Marie Brown

Text © 2004 by Ann Marie Brown.
All rights reserved.
Maps © 2004 by Avalon Travel Publishing.
All rights reserved.

Avalon Travel Publishing is a division of
Avalon Publishing Group, Inc.

Some photos are used by permission
and are the property of the original copyright owners.

ISBN: 1-56691-742-5
ISSN: 1545-5394

Editor: Marisa Solís
Series Manager: Marisa Solís
Copy Editor: Kimberly Spatz
Proofreader: Patrick Collins
Graphics Coordinator: Susan Snyder
Production Coordinator: Darren Alessi
Cover and Interior Design: Darren Alessi
Map Editor: Olivia Solís
Cartographers: Ben Pease, Kat Kalamaras, Mike Morgenfeld
Indexer: Kevin Millham

Front cover photo: © Ben Davidson/Robert Holmes Photography

Printed in the United States of America by Worzalla

Please send all feedback about this book to:

OGHORN OUTDOORS®
Bay Area Biking
Avalon Travel Publishing
1400 65th Street, Suite 250
Emeryville, CA 94608, USA
atpfeedback@avalonpub.com
www.foghorn.com

Printing History
1st edition—February 2004
5 4 3 2 1

ABOUT THE AUTHOR

The author of 12 outdoor guidebooks, Ann Marie Brown is a dedicated California outdoorswoman. She bikes, hikes, and camps more than 150 days each year in a dedicated effort to avoid routine, complacency, and getting a real job.

Ann Marie's love of bicycling was founded in her youth. At age 2, she commandeered her older sister's tricycle, pointed it down the steepest stretch of her family's driveway, and had her first experience with "road rash." She pedaled her first century tour at age 15, although the ride ended prematurely at mile 82 when her brakes failed on a steep descent in the rain. Fortunately, her bruises quickly healed, and her loving parents chipped in to buy her a new set of wheels. Ann Marie has been falling off one bike or another at regular intervals ever since. (She prefers the term "involuntary dismount.")

Ann Marie's work has appeared in *Sunset, VIA, Backpacker,* and *California* magazines. As a way of giving back a bit of what she gets from her outdoor experiences, she writes and edits for several environmental groups, including the Sierra Club and Natural Resources Defense Council.

When not riding or hiking along a California trail, Ann Marie can be found at her home on the San Francisco Bay Area coastline, counting whale spouts instead of working.

In addition to *Foghorn Outdoors Bay Area Biking,* Ann Marie's outdoor guidebooks include:

Foghorn Outdoors 101 Great Hikes of the San Francisco Bay Area
Foghorn Outdoors 250 Great Hikes in California's National Parks
Foghorn Outdoors California Waterfalls
Foghorn Outdoors Easy Biking in Northern California
Foghorn Outdoors Easy Camping in Southern California
Foghorn Outdoors Easy Hiking in Northern California
Foghorn Outdoors Easy Hiking in Southern California
Foghorn Outdoors Northern California Biking
Foghorn Outdoors Southern California Cabins & Cottages
Moon Handbooks Yosemite
Foghorn Outdoors California Hiking (with Tom Stienstra)

For more information on these titles, visit Ann Marie's website at www.annmariebrown.com.

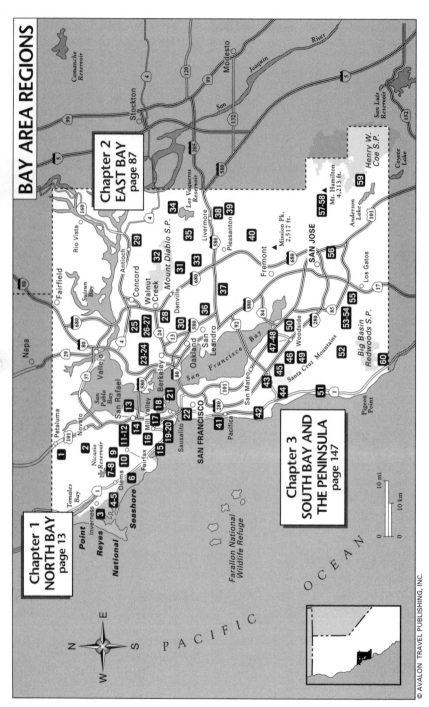

BAY AREA REGIONS

Chapter 1
NORTH BAY
page 13

Chapter 2
EAST BAY
page 87

Chapter 3
SOUTH BAY AND
THE PENINSULA
page 147

© AVALON TRAVEL PUBLISHING, INC.

CONTENTS

Chapter 1—North Bay

Chapter 3—South Bay and the Peninsula

🔲 = paved road or path   🔲 = dirt road or trail

Our Commitment

We are committed to making *Foghorn Outdoors Bay Area Biking* the most accurate and enjoyable guide to mountain biking and road cycling in the San Francisco Bay Area. Each ride has been carefully selected and tested so that we may offer readers the best of a variety of rides in the area. We've also incorporated nearby attractions and stops in each ride. Be aware, however, that with the passing of time, road conditions may have been upgraded (or downgraded), changes in weather may close trails, and featured attractions and bike shops may have moved. With these possibilities in mind, or if you have a specific need or concern, it's best to call the number(s) listed for the ride ahead of time.

If you would like to comment on the book, whether it's to suggest your favorite ride or to let us know about any noteworthy experience—good or bad—that occurred while using *Foghorn Outdoors Bay Area Biking* as your guide, we would appreciate hearing from you. Please address correspondence to:

Foghorn Outdoors Bay Area Biking
Avalon Travel Publishing
1400 65th Street, Suite 250
Emeryville, CA 94608

email: atpfeedback@avalonpub.com

If you send us an email, please put "Bay Area Biking" in the subject line. Thanks.

HOW TO USE THIS BOOK

Foghorn Outdoors Bay Area Biking is divided into three chapters: North Bay, East Bay, and South Bay and the Peninsula. Navigating this guide can be done easily in two ways:

1.
If you know the general area you want to visit, turn to the map at the beginning of this book. You can then determine which bike routes are in or near your destination by their corresponding numbers. Opposite the map, the table of contents lists each route by map number, name, and page number. Then turn to the corresponding page for the ride you're interested in.

2.
If you know the name of the route, or the name of the surrounding geographical area or nearby feature (town, park, forest, lake, etc.), look it up in the index and turn to the corresponding page.

About the Ride Number and Name
Each ride in this book has a number and name. The ride's number allows you to find it easily on the map. The name is either the actual trail or street name (as listed on signposts and maps) or a name I've given to a series of trails or streets. In these cases, the ride's name is taken from the focal point of the route, usually a geographic landmark, such as the name of a ridge it traverses or destination it reaches.

About the Route Details
Each ride is composed of one or more routes—the physical path that the ride takes. Here is where you'll find key information about the ride in five categories:

type of trail — This section notes the kind of trail surface(s) you'll encounter, plus how much car or other traffic is common along the route. Single-track trails are also noted here. Icons are used to provide at-a-glance information:

 = paved road or bike path; road bikes are appropriate

 = dirt road or trail; mountain bikes are appropriate

If both icons appear, the route is a mix of pavement and dirt; these routes are typically traveled by mountain bikes.

difficulty — This rating, from 1 to 5 water bottles (with 1 being the easiest), is determined by the amount of climbing required, the total mileage, and, for mountain bike rides, the trail surface and level of technical skill required. Other factors can also affect the rating, such as high-elevation air or extremely steep grades in sections of the route even when the total elevation gain is not exceptional. Changeable factors like hot weather can also make a relatively easy ride feel like a very difficult ride.

Thus, with a few modifications and adjustments, the scale is generally applied as follows:

🍶 🍶 🍶 🍶 🍶 — These rides would be suitable for families with young children, novice riders, or those wanting a casual, recreational ride for a little exercise and fresh air. They include both road and mountain bike rides that are nearly level (less than 500 feet of elevation gain) and less than 15 miles. Trail surfaces are smooth.

🍶 🍶 🍶 🍶 🍶 — These rides are suitable for families with older children and for strong beginners, i.e. novice riders who are physically fit. They include both road and mountain bike rides that have between 500 and 1,200 feet of elevation gain. Mountain bike trails are generally less than 15 miles; paved routes are generally less than 25 miles. Dirt trail surfaces may not be completely smooth, but they do not require any special skills for riding.

🍶 🍶 🍶 🍶 🍶 — These rides are suitable for road bike riders with solid aerobic fitness, and mountain bike riders with solid aerobic fitness and a moderate amount of experience on dirt trails, including single-track. They include both road and mountain bike rides that have between 1,200 and 2,000 feet of elevation gain. Mountain bike trails are generally less than 15 miles; paved routes are generally 25 to 50 miles. Dirt trail surfaces may require technical skills for riding, such as the ability to ride over and around rough surfaces (rocks, roots, or ruts), descend steep hills, maneuver through tight turns, follow a narrow line with good balance, etc.

🍶 🍶 🍶 🍶 🍶 — These rides are suitable for road bike riders with excellent aerobic fitness, and mountain bike riders with excellent aerobic fitness and substantial technical skills. They include both road and mountain bike rides that have between 2,000 and 3,500 feet of elevation gain. Mountain bike trails are generally less than 20 miles; paved routes are generally 25 to 50 miles, but with steeper climbs than rides rated 3. Dirt trail surfaces may require superior technical skills to handle steep descents, rocky terrain, etc.

iiiii — These are challenging rides for serious road cyclists. They include road rides having more than 3,500 feet of elevation gain. Routes are generally 50 or more miles.

total distance — This section conveys the total *round-trip* distance covered in miles.

riding time — This section conveys the total time it will take to complete the route for an adult with some biking experience in moderate shape. Riding times may vary due to level of experience, weather, and the number and length of any breaks taken.

elevation gain — This section conveys the approximate total elevation *climbed*. For example, if there are two peaks in a route, one with an 850-foot climb and the other with a 1,000-foot climb, the total elevation gain would be 1,850 feet. The measurements were taken using topographic maps and other paper sources. They may not be precise, but should be considered very good estimates.

About the Route Description

This narrative section outlines the less measurable elements of the ride. You'll read my observations about the ride in general, plus firsthand experience with other user groups, route conditions, and any technically difficult spots. How rain, wind, and heat can affect your ride is discussed, along with car traffic and any steep grades. I also describe the scenery and outstanding qualities of each ride.

About the Route Directions

With each ride in this book you'll find a mile-by-mile listing of what to expect along the trail or road. Every major junction or turn is noted in the mileage log and recorded to the nearest tenth of a mile. Please note, however, that determining mileage is an inexact science. One bicycle's cyclometer will often disagree with another bicycle's cyclometer. For example, reducing your tire pressure changes the rolling radius of your wheel, which affects what your cyclometer registers as mileage. Putting more weight on your front tire (such as during a descent) affects your cyclometer's reading. Then there is human error: Where you "zero out" your mileage (or where you start the clock) will have a big impact on your mile-by-mile status. Small diversions from the path (such as riding back 50 yards to check on your riding partner, then turning around and heading back) create noticeable changes in your mileage.

To put it simply, use some perspective when using the mileage logs. If the log notes that a right turn is coming up at mile 4.2 and you can't find it, try riding another quarter mile or so to see if it shows up (or backtrack, to see if you've missed it!). Most importantly, always carry a good map with you.

About the Elevation Profiles

Provided for each ride is an elevation profile, which approximately graphs the hills and dips on the route in height and distance. The scales on each profile are dramatically different, varying from 25-foot to 1,000-foot increments for height (elevation), and varying from a few miles to nearly 100 miles for distance. In addition, not all profiles begin at an elevation of zero feet. For this reason, please pay special attention to the numbers marked on the two axes of the graphs.

About the Maps

This book begins with a map of the region it covers. Every ride's starting point is noted by a number on the map. These points are placed as precisely as possible, but the scale of these maps often makes it difficult to pinpoint a ride's exact starting point. I advise that you purchase a detailed map of the area, especially if it is new to you.

All rides also feature a trail map. However, if the area is new to you, or if you would like maps showing topographic lines, I advise obtaining a more detailed map. If you are riding in a national, state, county, or regional park, obtain a park trail map from the visitor center or entrance station. If you are riding on the road, get a detailed AAA map of the area. Bike and outdoors shops also carry detailed maps.

MAP SYMBOLS

——	Road Route	○	City
⋯⋯	Unpaved Road Route	○	Town
‑ ‑ ‑	Trail Route	℗	Trailhead Parking
‑ ‑ ‑	Other Trail	**Start**	Start of Ride
⋯⋯⋯	Other Trail (Bikes Prohibited)	▪	Point of Interest
═══	Divided Highway	★	Natural Feature
═══	Primary Road	▲	Mountain
———	Secondary Road	⚑	State Park
⋯⋯⋯	Unpaved Road	⛺	Campground
		🝣	Waterfall

PREFACE

Whether your tastes run to fat tires or skinny tires, Campagnolo or Rock-shox, the San Francisco Bay Area is an undisputed mecca for cyclists. Home to thousands of pairs of well-toned legs, closets full of black Lycra shorts, and more than 100 bike shops, the City by the Bay and its surrounding landscape afford a world of opportunities for mountain bikers, road cyclists, and recreational riders of all types, including those pulling Burley trailers or sporting training wheels.

The Bay Area has all the right ingredients for cycling nirvana: hilly back roads, narrow and winding coastal Highway 1, world-famous landmarks like the Golden Gate Bridge, and even Mount Tamalpais, the self-proclaimed birthplace of mountain biking. It was on Mount Tam's steep slopes that Gary Fisher, Joe Breeze, and others held the first formal off-road bike races in the late 1970s. Those first bikes were heavy, clunky, and downright dangerous, but a few years and a few modifications later, mountain bike fever caught on and an industry was born.

Several park agencies around the Bay are particularly friendly to mountain bikers. We're fortunate to have the East Bay Regional Park District, Golden Gate National Recreation Area, and Midpeninsula Regional Open Space District on our side. Even Point Reyes National Seashore allows mountain bikes on many of its trails—a rarity in the national park system. Several state parks do, too: Mount Diablo, Mount Tamalpais, Big Basin Redwoods, Angel Island, McNee Ranch, Portola Redwoods, Henry Coe, and China Camp. A handful of these parks even allow bikers on some of their single-track trails, not just wide fire roads.

For a tamer ride, the San Francisco Bay Area is nationally recognized for its wealth of paved bike paths, most of which began as railroad right-of-ways. For the cyclists, there are countless miles of back roads that travel the lesser known regions between the Bay Area's traffic-clogged interstates and highways. The Bay Area has more scenic, paved routes to ride than one could complete in a lifetime. Set among natural features such as towering redwood forests, bucolic bay wetlands, and the rugged coastline south to Waddell Creek and north to the outer reaches of west Marin County, the San Francisco Bay Area is the most wild metropolitan area in the United States. Whether you choose to ride on road or trail, you'll be witness to an urban wilderness like no other.

© ANN MARIE BROWN

Introduction

INTRODUCTION

It used to be that bicyclists fell into two categories: road cyclists and mountain bikers. The former spent a lot of money on bikes that weighed less than a full water bottle and black Spandex tights that fit like a second skin. They joined cycling clubs and milled around with their compatriots at coffee shops on Sunday mornings, drinking lattes and studying road maps before the day's ride.

The latter saw themselves as rebels, riding fat-tire bikes that were often splattered with mud. They wore baggy shorts and hiking boots, and were frequently heard yelling "yahoo" (or something similar) as they cleaned a boulder-lined descent or bunny-hopped over a fallen log. They coined their own phrases, like "eat rocks" and "dual-boing suspension."

At different phases of my life, I have been a card-carrying member of one group or the other. I pedaled century rides on a 19-pound skinny-tire wonder—a jerry-rigged, hand-me-down relic that was coveted by other riders for its all-Campy components. I searched out long and winding country roads and rode them in the good company of friends. In my best moments, I felt like I was a member of the *peloton* riding in the Tour de France.

Then, after moving to San Francisco and later to Marin County, I switched over to mountain bikes and cruised around the hills and dales of Northern California. I learned the difference between serpentine and granite and schist, and what it feels like to ride on, over, and around those marvelous rocks. I spotted red-tailed hawks and golden eagles, and shared the trails with deer, bears, and bobcats. In my best moments, I felt like I was using a two-wheeled machine to get closer to nature, to travel farther than I could on foot and visit places where automobiles could not go.

It never occurred to me that the twain could ever meet—that my two bicycling selves could shake hands and coexist happily. But somewhere inside, a small voice was seeking integration. Why be one thing and not the other? Why not embrace the two biking sports as one? And so this book was born. To me, the beauty of bicycling is its wind-in-the-hair, feeling-like-a-kid-again euphoria, which can be achieved on either road or trail. It is knowing that no matter what ails you in the rest of life—monotonous job, unrequited love, too much housework—all you need do is get on your bike and pedal and everything will feel better.

The 60 rides in this book, plus multiple options and add-ons, celebrate the all-in-one joy of both road biking and mountain biking. Whether you own both types of bikes or only one or the other, you will find a wealth of rides in these pages that suit your desires and ability level.

Inevitably you'll also discover my personal biases for scenery and serenity. On trail rides, you'll find waterfalls, ocean views, redwood forests, and summit vistas. (I don't enjoy grinding out miles just for the sake of it.) On paved rides, you'll find more of the same, plus wide shoulders and as few cars as possible. (I don't like cars flying by at 60 mph, shaving my legs with hot exhaust.) My guiding rule for choosing bike routes is this: With every ride, on road or trail, I like to return home feeling like I've done something extraordinary with my day.

Happy riding to you.

"When I see an adult on a bicycle, I do not despair for the future of the human race." —H. G. Wells

BIKING TIPS

Biking Safety

Like the Boy Scout motto says, "Be prepared." It's easy to set off on a bike ride, especially near your home, carrying nothing except your wallet and keys. We've all done it from time to time. But even on the shortest spin through the neighborhood or local park it's wise to have a few items with you. Some riders carry all of the following items on every ride, some carry only some of the items some of the time. But each of these could prove to be a real lifesaver.

• **A helmet for your head.** They don't call them "brain buckets" for nothing. Don't get on your bike without one; many parks require them and the ones that don't, should. Just as you wear your seat belt when you drive, wear your helmet when you ride. Make sure yours fits properly and strap it on securely.

• **Food and water.** Being hungry or thirsty spoils a good time, and it can also turn into a potentially dangerous situation. Even if you aren't the least bit hungry or thirsty when you start, you will feel completely different after 30 minutes of riding. Always carry at least two water bottles on your bike, and make sure they are full of fresh, clean water when you head out. Add ice on hot days, if you wish. For a two- to three-hour ride, 100 ounces of water is not overkill, especially in summer. Many riders prefer to wear a bladder-style backpack hydration system, which has the extra advantage of providing room to carry a few snacks or car keys. Always bring some form of calories with you, even if it's just a couple of energy bars. If you carry extras to share, you'll be the hero or heroine when you give them to a rider in need.

• **Cycling gloves and cycling shorts.** These make your trip a lot more comfortable. Cycling gloves have padded palms so the nerves in your hands are protected from extensive pressure when you lean your upper body weight on the handlebars. Cycling shorts have chamois or other padding in the saddle area, and it's obvious what that does.

• **A map of the park or roads you are riding.** Sometimes trails and roads are signed, sometimes they're not. Signs get knocked down or disappear with alarming frequency, due to rain, wind, or souvenir hunters. Get a map from the managing agency of the park you're visiting; all their names and phone numbers are listed in this book. For road rides, take along a detailed AAA or other map for the region.

• **A bike repair kit.** How much and which tools to carry is a great subject of debate. At the very least, if you're going to be farther than easy walking distance from your car, carry what you need to fix a flat tire. Great distances are covered quickly on a bike. This is never more apparent than when a tire goes flat 30 minutes into a ride and it takes two hours to walk back. So why walk? Carry a spare tube, a patch kit, tire levers, and a bike pump attached to your bike frame. Make sure you know how to use them.

Many riders also carry a small set of metric wrenches, allen wrenches, and a couple of screwdrivers, or some type of all-in-one bike tool. These are good for adjusting derailleurs and the angle on your bike seat, making minor repairs, and fidgeting with brake and gear cables. If you're riding on dirt trails, carry extra chain lubricant with you, or at least keep some in your car. Some riders carry a few additional tools, such as a spoke wrench for tightening loose spokes, or a chain tool to fix a broken chain.

• **Extra clothing.** On the trail, weather and temperature conditions can change at any time. It may get windy or start to rain, or you can get too warm as you ride uphill in the sun and then too cold as you ride downhill in the shade. Wear layers. Bring a lightweight jacket and a rain poncho with you. Tie your extra clothes around your waist or put them in a small daypack.

• **Sunglasses and sunscreen.** Wear both. Put on your sunscreen 30 minutes before you go outdoors so it has time to take effect.

• **A bike lock.** It comes in handy if you want to stop for anything. Many of the trails in this book combine a bike ride with a short hike or a visit to a winery, museum, or historic site. If you are planning to stop anywhere, even to use a restroom, a bike lock is valuable. Never leave your bike unlocked and unattended.

• **First-aid kit and emergency money for phone calls.** See the next page for more details.

First Aid and Emergencies

Like most of life, bicycling is a generally safe activity that in the mere bat of an eye can suddenly become unsafe. The unexpected occurs—a rock in the trail, a sudden change in road surface, a misjudgment or momentary lack of attention—and suddenly, you and your bike are sprawled on the ground. Sooner or later it happens to everyone who rides. Usually, you look around nervously to see if anybody saw you, dust yourself off, and get back on your bike. But it's wise to carry a few emergency items just in case your accident is more serious: A few large and small Band-Aids, antibiotic cream, and an Ace bandage can be valuable tools. I also carry a Swiss Army knife, one with several blades, a can opener, and scissors. If I don't need it for first aid, I'll use it for bike repairs or picnics. Finally, it's a good idea to carry matches in a waterproof container and a candle, just in case you ever need to build a fire in a serious emergency.

Some riders carry a cell phone everywhere they go, but be forewarned that this is not a foolproof emergency device. You won't get cell reception in many areas, particularly in nonurban places. Carry a cell phone and hope it will work, but don't expect to rely on it.

Always bring along a few bucks so you can make a phone call from a pay phone, or buy food or drinks for yourself or someone who needs them.

Bike Maintenance

Most bike-related problems won't occur if you do a little upkeep on your machine. Remember to check your tire pressure, seat height, brakes, and shifters before you begin each ride. Lubricate your chain and wipe off the excess lubricant. Make sure all is well before you set out on the trail.

If you are riding often, you should also clean your bike and chain frequently, lubricate cables and derailleurs, tighten bolts, and check your wheels for alignment. Don't wait to have your bike worked on when you bring it into the shop occasionally; learn to perform your own regular maintenance and do it frequently.

Mountain Biking Etiquette

Mountain bikes are great. They give you an alternative to pavement, a way out of the concrete jungle. They guarantee your freedom from auto traffic. They take you into the woods and the wild, to places of natural beauty.

On the other hand, mountain bikes are the cause of a lot of controversy. In the past 15 years, mountain bikers have shown up on trails that were once the exclusive domain of hikers and horseback riders. Some say the peace and quiet has been shattered. Some say that trail surfaces are being ruined by the weight and force of mountain bikes. Some say that mountain bikes are too fast and clumsy to share the trail with other types of users.

Much of the debate can be resolved if bikers follow a few simple rules, and if nonbikers practice a little tolerance. The following are a list of rules for low-impact, "soft cycling." If you obey them, you'll help to give mountain biking the good name it deserves:

1. Ride only on trails where bikes are permitted. Obey all signs and trail closures.

2. Yield to equestrians. Horses can be badly spooked by bicyclists, so give them plenty of room. If horses are approaching you, stop alongside the trail until they pass. If horses are traveling in your direction and you need to pass them, call out politely to the rider and ask permission. If the horse and rider moves off the trail and the rider tells you it's okay, then pass.

3. Yield to hikers. Bikers travel much faster than hikers. Understand that you have the potential to scare the daylights out of hikers as you speed downhill around a curve and overtake them from behind, or race at them head-on. Make sure you give other trail users plenty of room, and keep your speed down when you are near them. If you see a hiker, slow down to a crawl, or even stop.

4. Be as friendly and polite as possible. Potential ill will can be eliminated by friendly greetings as you pass: "Hello, beautiful day today . . ." Always say thank you to other trail users for allowing you to pass.

5. Avoid riding on wet trails. Bike tires leave ruts in wet soil that accelerate erosion. This makes bikers very unpopular with park managers and other trail users.

6. Riders going downhill should always yield to riders going uphill on narrow trails. Get out of their way so they can keep their momentum as they climb.

Mountain Biking Basics

• First-time mountain bike riders are always surprised at how much time they spend walking instead of riding. They walk their bike up steep grades, down steep grades, and in level places where the terrain is too rugged. Mountain bikers frequently have to deal with rocks, boulders, tree roots, sand traps, holes in the ground, stream crossings, eroded trails, and so on. Often the best way to deal with these obstacles is to walk and push your bike.

• If something looks scary, dismount and walk. If you are unsure of your ability to stay in control while heading downhill, or your capacity to keep your balance on a rough surface, dismount and walk. It will save you plenty of Band-Aids.

• Learn to shift gears before you need to. This takes some practice, but you'll soon find that it's easier to shift before you're halfway up the hill and the pedals and chain are under pressure. When you see a hill coming up ahead, downshift.

• Play around with the height of your seat. When the seat is properly adjusted, you will have a slight bend in your knee while your leg is fully extended on the lower of the two pedals.

• Take it easy on the handlebar grips. Many beginners squeeze the daylights out of their handlebars, which leads to hand, arm, shoulder, and upper back discomfort. Grip the handlebars loosely and keep a little bend in your elbows.

• Learn to read the trail ahead of you, especially on downhills. Keep your eyes open for rocks or ruts, which can take you by surprise and upset your balance.

• Go slowly. As long as you never exceed the speed at which you feel comfortable and in control, you'll be fine. This doesn't mean that you shouldn't take a few chances, but it's unwise to take chances until you are ready.

• Experienced riders can maneuver their bikes on nearly any terrain. But, remember that good technical ability also means managing one's speed. Especially when riding on trails shared by hikers, dogs, and horses, it's important to use one's brakes wisely. Brake before you enter turns or corners so you can ride through them *without* braking. Braking during a turn or curve causes you to lock up your rear wheel and skid or slide. Sliding lessens your control over the bike and is very destructive to the trail. Ride it; don't slide it, or you'll make yourself very unpopular with people who love trails.

• Use the front brake simultaneously and in combination with the back brake to slow you down. But don't pull too hard on the front brake or you'll go over the handlebars. Remember that 70 percent of your braking force is in your front brake.

• Learn to move your weight back and lift up your front wheel to get it over obstacles, like rocks or bumps. Otherwise, your front wheel can get trapped, causing you to fly over the handlebars. Your back wheel will usually roll over obstacles.

• Lean inside and forward into turns and curves. This keeps your center of gravity over your tires.

• On downhills, get your rear end as far back on the bike as possible—behind the seat and over the back tire if you can.

• When you are approaching a long, steep downhill, stop for a moment and lower your seat. You want to be able to stand in a crouched position without the seat getting in the way.

• Never ride in mud; your tire tracks will encourage erosion. Walk your bike around muddy areas; don't ride around them and create another trail.

Protecting the Outdoors

Take good care of this beautiful land you're riding on. The primary rules are to leave no trace of your visit, to pack out all your trash, and to try not to disturb animal or plant life. But you can go the extra mile and pick up any litter that you see on the trail or road. Carry an extra bag to hold the litter you collect until you get to a trash receptacle, or just keep an empty pocket for that purpose.

If you have the extra time or energy, you can join a trail organization in your area or spend some time volunteering in your local park. Biking and hiking trails need constant upkeep and maintenance, and most of the work gets done by volunteers. Anything you do to help this lovely planet will be repaid to you, many times over.

BEST BIKE RIDES

Of the 60 road and trail rides in this book, here are my favorites in seven categories:

Best Rides for Families

Bear Valley Trail Bike & Hike, page 23. This excursion in Point Reyes National Seashore is easy enough for cyclists of any ability, and leads to a spectacular coastal overlook.

Berry Creek Falls Bike & Hike, page 209. An 11-mile round-trip bike ride in Big Basin State Park brings you to a short hike to one of the Bay Area's most spectacular waterfalls.

Cross Marin Trail/Sir Francis Drake Bikeway, page 36. Ride the old North Pacific Coast Railroad right-of-way through a forest of ferns and redwoods.

Nimitz Way & Wildcat Canyon, page 88. Perched on the tip of San Pablo Ridge in Tilden Park, Nimitz Way Trail offers the best views of any paved trail in the East San Francisco Bay.

Perimeter Trail & Fire Road Loops, page 79. This 5.5-mile, nearly level trail circumnavigates Angel Island in the middle of San Francisco Bay, providing outstanding views and some interesting history lessons.

Sawyer Camp Recreation Trail, page 154. This trail in the pristine San Francisco Watershed near Hillsborough travels the length of Lower Crystal Springs Reservoir and leads through marshlands to southern San Andreas Lake.

Best Rides through History

Old Stage Road & Old Railroad Grade to East Peak, page 63. Take a ride through Mount Tamalpais history on this eight-mile out-and-back on the old Mount Tamalpais Scenic Railway route, home of the "Crookedest Railroad in the World."

Perimeter Trail & Fire Road Loops, page 79. Visit the many remaining buildings on Angel Island, which has had a long and varied history as a military outpost, Russian sea otter hunters' site, and immigrant detention center.

Stewartville & Ridge Trail Loop, page 109. Pedal through Black Diamond Mines Regional Preserve, which from 1860 to 1906 was the site of the largest coal mining district in California.

Best Waterfront Rides

Cheese Company & Tomales Bay Loop, page 17. Stop for a lunch of fresh oysters as you pedal a nine-mile stretch alongside Tomales Bay.

© ANN MARIE BROWN

Golden Gate Bridge & Marin Headlands Loop, page 83. Ride across the Golden Gate Bridge, visit the Point Bonita Lighthouse, and stop at Black Sand and Rodeo Beaches on this remarkable coastal loop route.

Pescadero & San Gregorio Loop, page 179. Pedal south on coastal Highway 1 past Pigeon Point Lighthouse and Whaler's Cove, then loop back through the historic towns of Pescadero and San Gregorio.

Tiburon & Belvedere Loop, page 69. This easy road ride circles around the Tiburon Peninsula and Belvedere Island, passing multi-million-dollar homes and providing priceless bay views.

Best Rides for Wildlife Viewing

Stinson Beach & Mount Tamalpais Loop, page 60. From mid-March to mid-July, see hundreds of pairs of great egrets nesting in the trees at Bolinas Lagoon Preserve.

Point Reyes Lighthouse, page 26. From December to April, spot gray whales from the Point Reyes Lighthouse coastal promontory and observe elephant seals from an overlook at nearby Chimney Rock.

Alameda Creek Trail, page 144. You may notice a few birds as you ride alongside Alameda Creek, but when you reach the trail's end at Coyote Hills Regional Park and the San Francisco Bay National Wildlife Refuge, you're in some of the best birdwatching territory in the Bay Area.

Best Rides to High Overlooks

Montara Mountain, page 151. Pick a clear day for this mountain bike ride to the summit of 1,898-foot Montara Mountain, where you'll be rewarded with dazzling views of the Pacific coast.

Mount Diablo Summit Ride, page 122. You haven't experienced Mount

Diablo's Summit Road until you've ridden it on a bike—all the way to the mountain summit at 3,849 feet, where you can see as far as the Sierra Nevada.

Mount Hamilton, page 200. Climb to the top of the Bay Area's loftiest peak, Mount Hamilton at 4,209 feet, where astronomers at Lick Observatory keep a watch on the stars.

Stinson Beach & Mount Tamalpais Loop, page 60. Starting from sea level at Stinson Beach, ride to the 2,571-foot summit of Mount Tamalpais's East Peak on scenic back roads.

Best Single-Track

El Corte de Madera Creek Loop, page 162. A wide variety of trails, including plenty of challenging single-track, tunnel through a dense forest of redwoods and Douglas firs at this Skyline Boulevard open space preserve.

Middle Ridge Loop, page 206. It isn't easy riding in this steep, hilly park, but Henry Coe is known to have some of the best single-track in the Bay Area.

Saratoga Gap Loop, page 189. Peninsula mountain bikers head for this 12.9-mile loop through three contiguous parklands to sharpen their single-track skills.

Tamarancho Loop, page 46. You have to pay a few bucks for a permit to ride at the Boy Scouts' Camp Tamarancho near Fairfax, but this seven-mile single-track loop is well worth the fee.

Best Rides for Wine-Tasting

Big Basin & Boulder Creek Loop, page 186. Only two wineries are located on this strenuous 43-mile loop, but they are perfectly situated for taking a rest stop on the long climb up Bear Creek Road.

Livermore Winery Ride, page 140. In less than 20 miles of pedaling you can tour the rolling hills of Livermore and taste the products of nearly a dozen wineries.

Saratoga to Montebello Road Summit, page 193. Weekend wine tasting at Ridge Winery is the reward for the ascent up Montebello Road in area.

© ANN MARIE BROWN

Chapter 1

North Bay

1. PETALUMA & DILLON BEACH RAMBLE

Petaluma to Dillon Beach, northwest Marin County

Type of trail:  paved roads with minimal car traffic

Difficulty: ▮▮▮▯▯   **Total distance:** 55.3 miles (or 25-mile option)

Riding time: 4 hours   **Elevation gain:** 1,800 feet

Chileno Valley Road is the long, rambling way to get to the coast from Petaluma, but for bicyclists, it's the obvious choice. The road is filled with small ups and downs, multiple curves and twists, and a whole lot of cows standing beside it and sometimes in it. Few motorists bother with this road; they use the more direct Bodega Avenue instead.

After a 12.6-mile stint on Chileno Valley's bucolic, pasture-lined thoroughfare, this rambling ride makes a loop through the small towns of Valley Ford, Dillon Beach, and Tomales. This results in a perfect half-day ride with no killer climbs, but with plenty of great scenery, both in the inland hills and on the windswept coast.

Each of these three towns has an interesting history. Valley Ford was a

Pasture-lined Chileno Valley Road is the rambler's way from Petaluma to the coast.

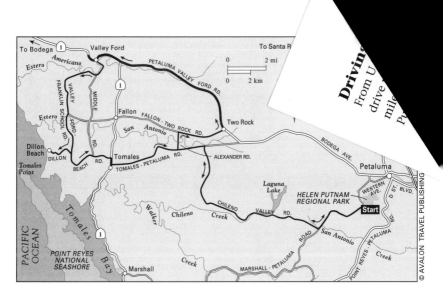

potato-farming community in the 19th century, but in the 1920s the residents took up sheep farming. Little has changed since then; you'll still see plenty of woolly sheep, plus an abundance of cows and a smattering of llamas. Dillon Beach has been a seaside resort since 1888, when George Dillon constructed a hotel at the end of the West Marin railroad line, hoping to attract city folk to the local beaches and clamming beds. Tomales was a railroad stop in the late 1880s. Today its short main street boasts a general store, a wonderful bakery that is always worthy of a stop, a café, and a restaurant.

If the mileage on this ride seems intimidating, it is easy enough to cut it into two rides for two separate days: a 25-mile out-and-back on Chileno Valley Road starting from Helen Putnam Regional Park, and a 27-mile loop through Tomales, Dillon Beach, and Valley Ford, starting from any of those towns.

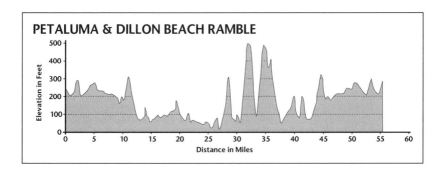

Directions

S. 101 in Petaluma, take the Petaluma Boulevard South exit and north two miles. Turn left (west) on Western Avenue and drive 2.2 s, then turn left on Chileno Valley Road and drive .8 mile to Helen tnam Regional Park on the left.

Route Directions for Petaluma & Dillon Beach Ramble

0.0 Park at Helen Putnam Regional Park and ride west on Chileno Valley Road. (Parking is available inside the park or in pullouts along the road.) *Supplies are available in Petaluma.*

3.0 RIGHT to stay on Chileno Valley Road.

12.6 LEFT on Tomales-Petaluma Road.

13.8 RIGHT on Alexander Road.

14.8 RIGHT on Fallon-Two Rock Road.

17.2 LEFT on Petaluma-Valley Ford Road (hamlet of Two Rock).

26.0 LEFT on Valley Ford Estero Road (town of Valley Ford). *Supplies are available.*

31.8 RIGHT on Dillon Beach Road. Ride out and back through Dillon Beach, then TURN AROUND and return to junction with Valley Ford Road. *Supplies are available in Dillon Beach.*

34.6 RIGHT on Dillon Beach Road.

37.2 RIGHT on Shoreline Highway (Highway 1) in town of Tomales. *Supplies are available.*

37.5 LEFT on Tomales-Petaluma Road.

42.7 RIGHT on Chileno Valley Road.

52.3 LEFT to stay on Chileno Valley Road.

55.3 Arrive at starting point.

2. CHEESE COMPANY & TOMALES BAY LOOP

Novato to Marshall, northwest Marin County

Type of trail: paved roads with minimal car traffic

Difficulty: ▐▐▐▐▐   **Total distance:** 46 miles

Riding time: 3–4 hours   **Elevation gain:** 1,800 feet

This is a ride for the gourmet cyclist. You'll work up an appetite on this 46-mile ride, then satisfy it with barbecued oysters from Tomales Bay and brie and camembert from the Marin French Cheese Company (707/762-6001).

Although Marin County has many scenic road rides, this is one of the loveliest. It offers a mix of pastoral hills and green, fertile valleys, plus level riding along the edge of Tomales Bay. The bucolic charms of this ride will make you forget you are in the same county (perhaps even the same country) as the busy corridor of U.S. 101 north of the Golden Gate.

Plus, the loop visits two of west Marin's most charming towns: Marshall and Point Reyes Station. Marshall is known for two things: tranquil

cranking up the start of Marshall-Petaluma Road's demanding two-mile climb

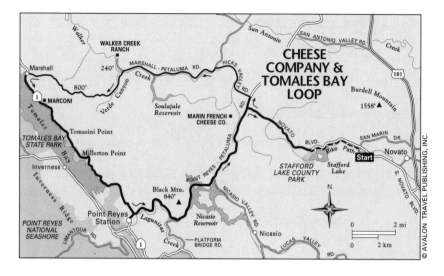

bay views and shellfish. More than half of California's oyster and shellfish growers lease acreage on the floor of Tomales Bay. To sample the local mollusks, head for either Hog Island or Tomales Bay Oyster Companies.

Point Reyes Station is three-tenths of a mile off the loop. The old railroad town features an eclectic mix of shops and cafés that cater to visitors at nearby Point Reyes National Seashore.

The ride has two major hills you should be warned about. The first is a two-mile brutal stint on Marshall-Petaluma Road. Although the seldom-traveled road is a beauty, with lots of ups, downs, and winding curves, its one major hill is infamous for bringing cyclists to their knees. Know in advance that the hardest climbing takes place from mile 15.9 to 17.5, in an area called Three Peaks.

With that ascent accomplished, your reward is a euphoric descent to the coast at Marshall, where after snacking on a half-dozen oysters, you'll enjoy nine miles of gentle pedaling along the edge of Tomales Bay. This is some exquisite water's-edge scenery, and if you're lucky enough to ride it on a weekday, you'll contend with fewer cars on Highway 1.

After your bayside stint, you can opt for a brief side trip into Point Reyes Station, or just head inland for the final leg to the Marin French Cheese Company. On this stretch, you'll face the second big hill, about a mile past Nicasio Reservoir. The ascent is sustained over 1.5 miles, but it's not as bad as the Marshall-Petaluma hill because you know a big round of brie is waiting on the other side. Be sure to take the Cheese Company's factory tour so you can learn how the yummy stuff is made. *Bon appétit.*

Driving Directions

From San Rafael, drive north for 10 miles on U.S. 101 and take the San Marin Drive exit. Drive northwest for 2.7 miles to the intersection of San Marin Drive and Novato Boulevard, where the bike path begins.

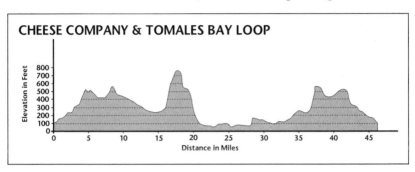

Route Directions for Cheese Company & Tomales Bay Loop

0.0 Park at the intersection of San Marin Drive and Novato Boulevard in Novato, then ride west on the bike path that parallels Novato Boulevard. *Supplies are available in Novato.*

2.5 Pass Stafford Lake County Park on the left; bike trail ends and you ride on Novato Boulevard. *Water is available.*

6.2 RIGHT on Petaluma-Point Reyes Road.

6.7 LEFT on Hicks Valley Road.

9.4 LEFT on Marshall-Petaluma Road.

15.9 Start of steepest climb.

17.5 Summit.

20.3 LEFT on Highway 1 in Marshall. *Supplies are available; stop at Tony's Seafood or Hog Island Oyster Company.*

24.3 Tomales Bay Oyster Company on right.

25.1 Tomales Bay State Park/Millerton Point beach and picnic area.

29.2 LEFT on Petaluma-Point Reyes Road. *Or go right to head into town of Point Reyes Station in .3 mile.*

33.1 LEFT at junction with Platform Bridge Road.

33.9 Pass Nicasio Reservoir.

39.3 LEFT into Marin French Cheese Company parking lot. *Tours of the cheese factory are available from 10 A.M. to 4 P.M. daily; supplies are available.*

39.7 RIGHT on Novato Boulevard.

43.5 Pick up bike trail at Stafford Lake County Park.

46.0 Arrive at starting point.

3. ESTERO TRAIL

Point Reyes National Seashore

Type of trail:  dirt road and single-track

Difficulty: ▮▮▯▯▯

Total distance: 12 miles

Riding time: 3 hours

Elevation gain: 1,200 feet

The Estero Trail is quintessential Point Reyes. It's full of good surprises, including an exemplary display of Douglas iris in spring; a dense Monterey pine forest; ample bird-watching opportunities; nonstop views of estuary, bay, and ocean; and access to a pristine beach and high bluff-top overlook. Pack a lunch and binoculars and plan on an unhurried ride to fully enjoy this excursion.

From the parking lot, the trail laterals across a grassy hillside, then rounds a corner and descends into a dense stand of Monterey pines, the tall and aged remains of an old Christmas tree farm and the nesting site of owls and egrets. Shortly the trail opens out to blue, serene Home Bay. A bridge crossing leads you to the first of several short climbs, this one rewarding you with high views of Home Bay's junction with Drakes Estero.

The ride continues parallel to the estero, with nonstop water views. If the tide is out, mud flats and the oyster beds of nearby Johnson's Oyster Farm

Estero Trail crosses a bridge over Home Bay, then parallels the edge of Drakes Estero.

will be revealed. If the tide is in, you'll see miles of azure water. You'll climb and descend a total of three hills on this trail; the third one has a lone eucalyptus tree growing on its summit.

At 2.5 miles, a sign marks Drakes Head to the left and Sunset Beach straight ahead. Turn left and climb through grasslands and chaparral to a confusing maze of cattle gates and fences (watch for arrow signs along the fence). Drakes Head Trail continues southward; the path crosses a coastal prairie and ends on a high bluff overlooking the ocean and Limantour Spit, a long, narrow stretch of sand and bluffs.

Returning to the junction, take Sunset Beach Trail. The path levels and in 1.5 miles you are within view of Sunset Beach. A large, quiet pond separates it from you, and the trail becomes mucky and impassable for bike tires. Stash your bike and explore beautiful Sunset Beach on foot.

For more information, contact Point Reyes National Seashore, 415/ 464-5100.

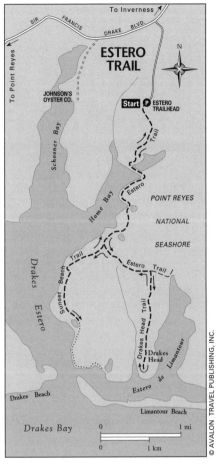

Driving Directions

From San Francisco, cross the Golden Gate Bridge and drive north on U.S. 101 for 7.5 miles. Take the Sir Francis Drake Boulevard exit west toward San Anselmo, and drive 20 miles to the town of Olema. At Olema, turn right (north) on Highway 1 for about 150 yards, then turn left on Bear Valley Road. Drive 2.2 miles on Bear Valley Road until it joins with Sir Francis Drake Highway. Bear left on Sir Francis Drake and drive 7.6 miles to the left turnoff for the Estero Trailhead. Turn left and drive one mile to the trailhead parking on the right.

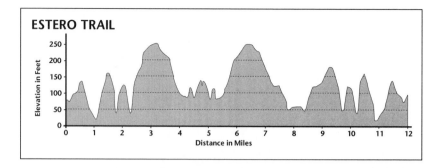

ESTERO TRAIL

Elevation in Feet / Distance in Miles

Route Directions for Estero Trail

0.0 Park at Estero Trailhead. *Supplies are available in the town of Inverness on Sir Francis Drake Highway.*

1.1 Bridge across Home Bay.

2.5 LEFT at junction with Drakes Head Trail (Sunset Beach Trail continues straight).

2.8 Maze of cattle gates, fences, and hiker gates; follow the fenceline path signed with arrows.

3.2 RIGHT on Drakes Head Trail; trail becomes indistinct in places—keep heading south toward the bluff's edge.

4.5 Drakes Head overlook. TURN AROUND.

6.5 LEFT on Sunset Beach Trail at previous junction.

8.0 Arrive at edge of pond with Sunset Beach beyond; stash your bike and explore on foot. TURN AROUND.

12.0 Arrive at starting point.

4. BEAR VALLEY TRAIL BIKE & HIKE

Point Reyes National Seashore

Type of trail: dirt road

Difficulty: 🍾🍾🍾🍾🍾   **Total distance:** 6.2 miles (plus 1.8-mile hike)

Riding time: 2 hours   **Elevation gain:** 500 feet

Don't forget your bike lock for this easy, scenic ride in Point Reyes National Seashore (415/464-5100). You'll ride for 3.1 miles, then hike almost a mile to the top of Arch Rock, a spectacular coastal overlook. Because of this trail's well-deserved popularity, time your trip for a weekday or an early morning on the weekend. It's more fun to ride if you aren't dodging a crowd of bikers and hikers.

Beginning just past the Bear Valley Visitor Center and Morgan Horse Ranch, the wide dirt trail is simple to follow. Several side trails intersect Bear Valley Trail but none are open to bikes. Just stay on the main path and cruise through the shady forest canopy, a dense mix of alders, laurel, fir, and bay. At the midway point, after the only noticeable climb of the ride, you'll reach grassy Divide Meadow, a popular picnic spot. Deer are common.

the final steps to Arch Rock on the Bear Valley Trail Bike & Hike

At 3.1 miles you come to a bike rack and several trail junctions. Lock up your bike and continue on foot to Arch Rock. The trail continues through the woods for .5 mile, following Coast Creek, then suddenly opens out to coastal marshlands. The final steps of the hike are extremely dramatic as you walk along the top of Arch Rock's jagged, jade-green bluff, which juts out over the sea. The wind can howl with tremendous fury out here—quite a surprise after the protected forest trail.

A spur trail leads down the cliffs to the beach; it's worth hiking during low tide when you can crawl through the tunnel of Arch Rock and explore the beach. Many visitors are content to stay on top of Arch Rock and enjoy the view of the surging waters below. If luck is with you, you'll catch sight of a passing gray whale, or at least a couple sea lions.

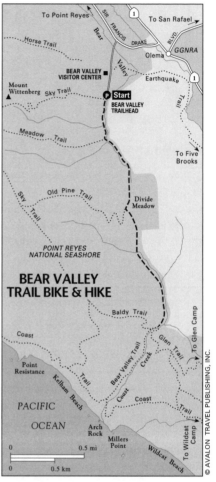

Driving Directions

From San Francisco, cross the Golden Gate Bridge and drive north on U.S. 101 for 7.5 miles. Take the Sir Francis Drake Boulevard exit west toward San Anselmo, and drive 20 miles to the town of Olema. At Olema, turn right (north) on Highway 1 for about 150 yards, then turn left on Bear Valley Road. Drive .5 mile, then turn left at the sign for Seashore Headquarters Information. Drive .25 mile and park in the large lot on the left, past the visitor center. Start riding along the park road, heading for the signed Bear Valley Trail.

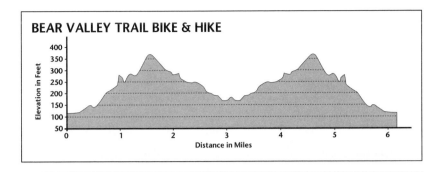

BEAR VALLEY TRAIL BIKE & HIKE

Route Directions for Bear Valley Trail Bike & Hike

0.0 Park at Bear Valley Trailhead just past the visitor center. Ride west on the continuation of the park road, which turns to dirt at a wide gate. *Supplies are available less than a mile away in the town of Olema; water is available at the visitor center.*

1.6 Divide Meadow.

3.1 Bike rack and junction with Glen, Baldy, and Bear Valley trails; TURN AROUND. *Lock up your bike and hike .9 mile on Bear Valley Trail to Arch Rock (straight ahead).*

6.2 Arrive at starting point.

5. POINT REYES LIGHTHOUSE

Point Reyes National Seashore

Type of trail: paved roads with moderate car traffic

Difficulty: 🥾🥾🥾🥾🥾 (4 if windy)   **Total distance:** 45 miles

Riding time: 3.5–4.5 hours   **Elevation gain:** 1,900 feet

Road cycling in Point Reyes National Seashore (415/464-5100) can be heavenly if the weather gods are on your side. If they aren't, you could face headwinds of 40-plus miles per hour, or fog so thick you miss all the scenery the park has to offer.

Remember this: Autumn and spring days are the surest bets for clear weather. Winter isn't bad, either, and that's when you have the best chance of spotting migrating whales from the park's shores. This road tour travels to two of the park's best whale-watching spots, the Point Reyes Lighthouse and Chimney Rock, and detours to gastronomic delights at Drake's Beach Cafe (415/669-1297) and Johnson's Oyster Company (415/669-1149).

From the Bear Valley Visitor Center, the route follows Bear Valley Road to Sir Francis Drake Highway and the bayside town of Inverness. Then Sir Francis Drake heads northwest into the park, leaving most of civilization behind with a short-but-steep ascent up and over Inverness Ridge. The ride continues on Sir Francis Drake as it threads through fields of colorful wild radish and acres of cow pastures to the western tip of Point Reyes National Seashore.

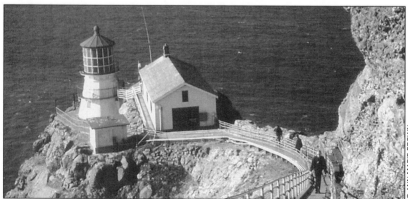

A visit to the lighthouse is one highlight of a road ride in Point Reyes.

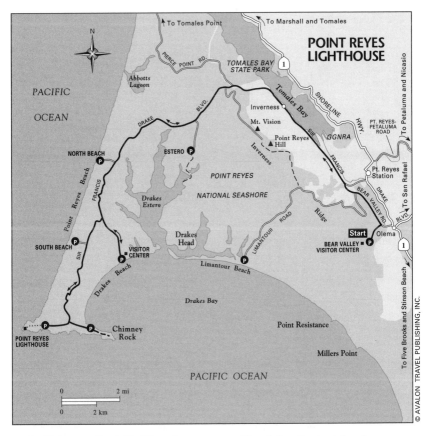

At Chimney Rock Trailhead, you can walk a 1.5-mile stretch where more than 60 species of wildflowers bloom on a narrow, windswept headland jutting into Drake's Bay, or look for elephant seals and gray whales in winter or spring. The ride finishes out at Point Reyes Lighthouse, where 300-plus steps descend to this breathtaking coastal promontory. To tour the lighthouse, plan your trip for Thursday through Monday; it's closed year-round on Tuesday and Wednesday.

Driving Directions

From San Francisco, cross the Golden Gate Bridge and drive north on U.S. 101 for 7.5 miles. Take the Sir Francis Drake Boulevard exit west toward San Anselmo, and drive 20 miles to the town of Olema. At Olema, turn right (north) on Highway 1 for about 150 yards, then turn left on Bear Valley Road. Drive .5 mile, then turn left at the sign for Seashore Headquarters Information. Drive .25 mile and park by the visitor center.

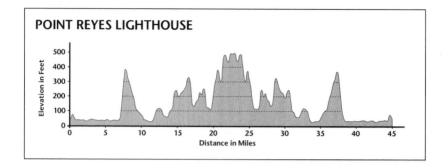

POINT REYES LIGHTHOUSE

Route Directions for Point Reyes Lighthouse

0.0 Park at Bear Valley Visitor Center, then ride back out the park road the way you came in. *Water is available at the visitor center.*

0.2 LEFT on Bear Valley Road.

1.8 LEFT on Sir Francis Drake Highway.

5.9 Town of Inverness. *Supplies are available.*

7.4 LEFT at Y-junction with Pierce Point Road.

8.7 STRAIGHT at junction with Mount Vision Road.

9.4 STRAIGHT at junction with Estero Trailhead Road.

10.4 Johnson's Oyster Company entrance on left. *If the oyster company is open, stop in for a grown-in-Point Reyes snack.*

13.2 STRAIGHT at junction for North Beach.

15.1 RIGHT at junction with Kenneth C. Patrick Visitor Center and Drake's Beach (save the left fork for your return trip).

19.4 LEFT at access road for Chimney Rock Trailhead.

20.3 Chimney Rock Trailhead. TURN AROUND. *Hike or mountain bike the 1.5-mile Chimney Rock Trail in winter for whale-watching and in spring for wildflowers. From December to April, walk a few hundred yards to the Elephant Seal Overlook to see the seals hauled out on Drakes Beach.*

21.2 LEFT on Sir Francis Drake Highway.

21.8 Point Reyes Lighthouse parking lot. TURN AROUND. *Tour the lighthouse and neighboring visitor center.*

26.7 RIGHT for Kenneth C. Patrick Visitor Center and Drake's Beach.

28.3 Drake's Beach parking lot. TURN AROUND. *The visitor center features fascinating exhibits on local history, flora, and fauna. Drake's Beach Cafe serves food every weekend and most weekdays.*

29.9 RIGHT on Sir Francis Drake Highway.

45.0 Arrive at starting point.

6. STEWART TRAIL

Point Reyes National Seashore

Type of trail:  dirt road

Difficulty: 𝐈𝐈𝐈𝐈◌

Total distance: 13 miles

Riding time: 2–3 hours

Elevation gain: 2,300 feet

Few national parks permit bikes on their trails, and even fewer allow bike-in camping at remote campgrounds. Point Reyes National Seashore (415/464-5100) is a rare exception, and Stewart Trail from Five Brooks Trailhead is your ticket to two backcountry camps in Point Reyes: Glen and Wildcat. Those wishing to bike-backpack can make a reservation and get a permit for one of the camps. Riders looking for a challenging day-time sojourn will also enjoy pedaling Stewart Trail.

Be prepared for some climbing; this is an aerobically strenuous ride with a long ascent in both directions of the out-and-back. The initial climb begins a quarter mile from the parking lot and makes a steady 1,200-foot ascent over 3.5 miles to a ridge called Fir Top. The name is

Stewart Trail provides a challenging day trip or the chance for an overnight bike-packing ride in Point Reyes National Seashore.

apt—the area is completely shaded by Douglas firs. Then Stewart Trail drops steeply toward the ocean, losing all that hard-won elevation, plus another 100 feet. At 5.2 miles is the turnoff for Glen Camp, where some riders spend the night. Stewart Trail continues downhill to the coast and Wildcat Camp. As you descend, be sure to give your brakes a rest now and then by stopping to enjoy occasional peeks at the ocean through the trees. And keep in mind that you'll face this slope in the uphill direction on your way home.

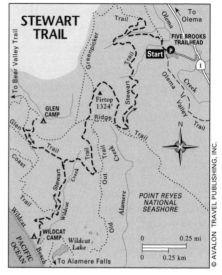

Stewart Trail ends 6.5 miles out at Wildcat Camp. Day visitors and campers alike will want to lock up their wheels and head to the neighboring beach to explore. If you're burning with energy, an option is to hike two miles south on Coast Trail (bikes are not allowed) to visit Alamere Falls, one of the Bay Area's loveliest waterfalls. The fall drops 50 feet over a coastal bluff to the sea.

Driving Directions

From San Francisco, cross the Golden Gate Bridge and drive north on U.S. 101 for 7.5 miles. Take the Sir Francis Drake Boulevard exit west toward San Anselmo, and drive 20 miles to the town of Olema. At Olema, turn left (south) on Highway 1 for 3.5 miles to Five Brooks Trailhead on the right.

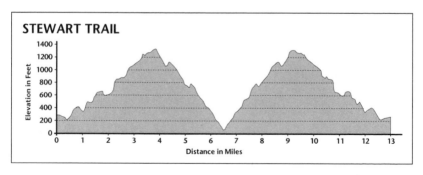

Route Directions for Stewart Trail

0.0 Park at Five Brooks Trailhead. Ride out the paved road past a large pond. *Supplies are available 3.5 miles away in the town of Olema; water is available at the trailhead.*

0.2 RIGHT on wide Stewart Trail.

3.0 RIGHT to stay on Stewart Trail at junction with Ridge Trail.

3.8 Arrive at Fir Top summit at 1,324 feet.

5.2 LEFT to stay on Stewart Trail at junction with Glen Trail (campers staying at Glen Camp turn right here).

6.5 Arrive at Wildcat Camp; TURN AROUND. *Lock up your bike and visit neighboring Wildcat Beach, or take a two-mile hike south on Coast Trail to Alamere Falls.*

13.0 Arrive at starting point.

7. BOLINAS RIDGE LOOP

Golden Gate National Recreation Area near Olema

7A (loop with Randall Trail)

Type of trail: 🐎 dirt road

Difficulty: 🚲🚲 🍶🍶🍶   **Total distance:** 15 miles (or shorter options)

Riding time: 2 hours   **Elevation gain:** 1,000 feet

7B (loop with Bolinas-Fairfax Road)

Type of trail: 🐎 🚵 dirt road and paved roads with minimal car traffic

Difficulty: 🚲🚲🚲🚲🍶   **Total distance:** 26 miles

Riding time: 4 hours   **Elevation gain:** 2,200 feet

The first time you ride Bolinas Ridge, you wonder how a trail could go up and down so much without ever leveling out. The path seems to have no pedal-and-cruise sections; you are either climbing up or coasting down the whole way (more of the latter than the former). The ridge's roller-

Open pasturelands line the northern edge of Bolinas Ridge near Olema.

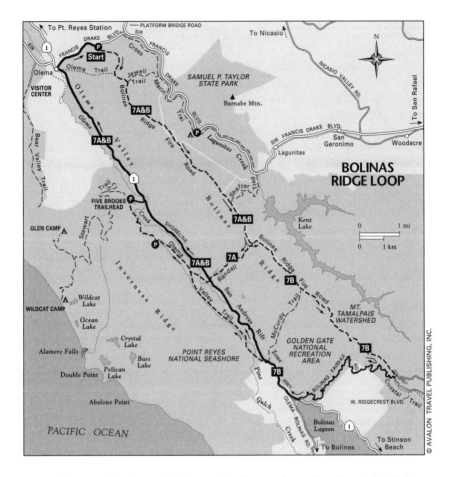

coastering grassland terrain is just plain fun, and scenic to boot: Its high points afford expansive views of Bolinas Lagoon to the south and Tomales Bay to the north. The trail is well-suited for all levels of riders; beginners can go out and back for a few miles while more advanced riders can choose from a variety of loops.

The key is to start on the Olema side of Bolinas Ridge at the Sir Francis Drake Highway trailhead, rather than on the Mount Tamalpais side at the Bolinas-Fairfax Road trailhead. From the Olema side, less ambitious riders can pedal southward for a handful of miles as the trail climbs moderately. The route carves through open pasturelands until the 5.4-mile mark, where it suddenly enters a thick Douglas fir and redwood forest. Say good-bye to the sun and the views and hello to the refreshing woods. When you've had enough and are ready to turn around and head home, a fun descent awaits.

Meanwhile, those with more energy can continue southeast on Bolinas Ridge and then loop around to Highway 1 on one of two steep downhill routes: Randall Trail at 6.2 miles out or paved Bolinas Fairfax Road at 11.1 miles out. The second half of either loop is an easy cruise northward on mostly level Highway 1 back to Olema. Your car awaits one mile up Sir Francis Drake Highway.

If the idea of riding on pavement insults your mountain biking sensibilities, you can omit a few road miles by riding dirt Olema Valley Trail, which runs parallel to Highway 1 from Dogtown to Five Brooks Trailhead. This is a dry-season option only, however: Olema Valley Trail is notorious for flooding with even the slightest rain.

Note that much of Bolinas Ridge is cattle country, so you'll have to lift your bike over several livestock gates in the first couple miles of trail. Be sure to leave every gate the way you found it, either open or closed.

For more information, contact Golden Gate National Recreation Area, 415/331-1540 or visit their website at www.nps.gov/goga.

Driving Directions

From San Francisco, cross the Golden Gate Bridge on U.S. 101 and travel north toward San Rafael. Take the Sir Francis Drake Boulevard exit west toward San Anselmo, and drive 19.5 miles to the trailhead for the Bolinas Ridge Trail on the left side of the road. If you reach the town of Olema and Highway 1, you've gone one mile too far.

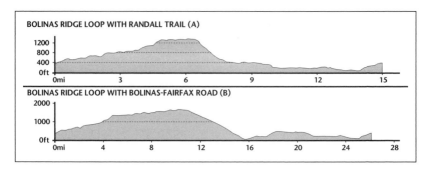

Route Directions for Bolinas Ridge Loop7A (loop with Randall Trail)

0.0 Park at the Bolinas Ridge trailhead pullout alongside Sir Francis Drake Highway, 1 mile northeast of Olema. Ride uphill and veer left onto the wide dirt road. *Supplies are available in Olema.*

1.4 RIGHT at junction with Jewell Trail to stay on Bolinas Ridge.

5.2 STRAIGHT at junction with Shafter Trail.

6.2 RIGHT at junction with Randall Trail.

7.9 RIGHT at junction with Highway 1.

14.0 RIGHT at junction with Sir Francis Drake in Olema.

15.0 Arrive at starting point.

Route Directions for 7B (loop with Bolinas-Fairfax Road)

Follow directions for Ride 7A to the 6.2-mile mark, then continue:

6.2 STRAIGHT at junction with Randall Trail.

7.8 STRAIGHT at junction with McCurdy Trail.

9.4 High point of Bolinas Ridge at 1,700 feet.

11.1 RIGHT at junction with Bolinas Fairfax Road.

15.6 RIGHT at junction with Highway 1.

25.0 RIGHT at junction with Sir Francis Drake in Olema.

26.0 Arrive at starting point.

8. CROSS MARIN TRAIL/ SIR FRANCIS DRAKE BIKEWAY

Samuel P. Taylor State Park near Olema

8A (Bike Path Only)

Type of trail: dirt road and paved bike path

Difficulty: 𝐼 𝐼 𝐼 𝐼 𝐼   **Total distance:** 10 miles (6 miles are paved)

Riding time: 1 hour   **Elevation gain:** 350 feet

8B (Loop with Bolinas Ridge Trail)

Type of trail: dirt road and paved bike path

Difficulty: 𝐼 𝐼 𝐼 𝐼 𝐼   **Total distance:** 13.4 miles

Riding time: 2.5 hours   **Elevation gain:** 1,250 feet

The Cross Marin Trail/Sir Francis Drake Bikeway is one trail with two names, under two different park jurisdictions. It's called the Cross Marin Trail when it's on Golden Gate National Recreation Area (415/331-1540) land, and the Sir Francis Drake Bikeway when it's on

The paved Sir Francis Drake Bikeway is lined with redwood needles and bordered by an abundance of ferns.

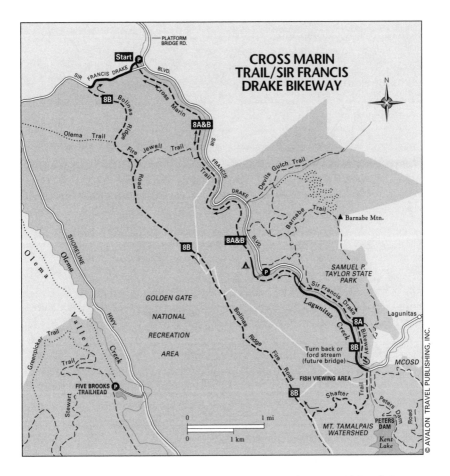

CROSS MARIN
TRAIL/SIR FRANCIS
DRAKE BIKEWAY

Samuel P. Taylor State Park (415/488-9897 or 415/893-1580) land. Two names, one trail.

The ride offers something for skinny tires and fat tires alike, with three miles of smooth pavement and another two miles of gravel and dirt suitable for mountain bikes. While plenty of people ride out and back on the bike path only (Ride 8A), others make a more strenuous loop by joining with Bolinas Ridge Trail (Ride 8B).

The bike path is an old rail trail, built in 1874 by the North Pacific Coast Railroad. Its first section is heavily wooded as it travels parallel to Papermill Creek, then opens out to a broad meadow. The path then heads back into the trees, entering dense second-growth redwood stands surrounded by prolific sorrel and ferns.

At the state park border, your primeval redwood fantasy gets rudely interrupted by campgrounds, restrooms, and other indicators of civilization. Where the paved surface erodes to gravel and dirt past Redwood Grove Picnic Area, skinny tires must turn around but mountain bikers continue riding, crossing a footbridge over Sir Francis Drake Highway. The trail ends two miles later at the park boundary, where Shafter Bridge arches over Papermill Creek.

But loop riders won't be discouraged by the abrupt trail ending. If the creek level is low enough, carry your bike across, then climb uphill to Shafter Bridge. (If the stream is too high to ford, backtrack and ride on Sir Francis Drake Highway from the park entrance to Shafter Bridge.) Next comes a gnarly, 1.8-mile winding climb up Shafter Bridge Fire Road that slays even the best of 'em (1,100-foot gain). At the top, a heavenly, mostly downhill cruise on Bolinas Ridge Road awaits. Where the ridge trail ends at Sir Francis Drake Highway, cruise down the paved road back to your car.

Driving Directions

From San Francisco, cross the Golden Gate Bridge on U.S. 101 and drive north for 7.5 miles. Take the Sir Francis Drake Boulevard exit west toward San Anselmo and drive 18.7 miles to the right turnoff for Platform Bridge Road, located 3.4 miles past the main entrance to Samuel P. Taylor State Park. (If you reach the town of Olema and Highway 1, you have gone 1.8 miles too far.) Turn right on Platform Bridge Road and park in the pullout on the left.

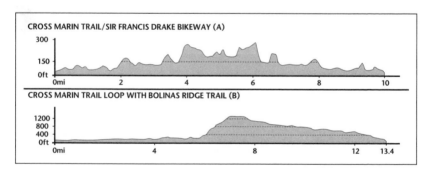

Route Directions for Cross Marin Trail/Sir Francis Drake Bikeway 8A (Bike Path Only)

0.0 Park at the Platform Bridge Road trailhead. Ride on the paved path leading from the pullout, cross a concrete bridge, go about 50 feet, then turn left on the signed Cross Marin Trail. *Supplies are available in Olema, two miles west.*

1.5 STRAIGHT at junction with Jewell Trail.

2.7 State park camping and picnic areas. *Water is available.*

3.0 Pavement ends; skinny tires must turn around.

3.4 Cross bridge over Sir Francis Drake Highway.

5.0 Trail ends at Papermill Creek and base of Shafter Bridge. TURN AROUND.

10.0 Arrive at starting point.

Route Directions for 8B (Loop with Bolinas Ridge Trail)

Follow the route directions for 8A to mile 5.0, then continue:

5.0 Ford the stream and climb up to the bridge.

5.2 Take Shafter Bridge Fire Road uphill (road on right side of creek).

7.0 RIGHT on Bolinas Ridge Trail at end of climb.

12.2 RIGHT on paved Sir Francis Drake Highway at end of Bolinas Ridge Trail.

13.3 LEFT on Platform Bridge Road.

13.4 Arrive at starting point.

9. NICASIO RESERVOIR LOOP

western Marin County

Type of trail:  paved roads with moderate car traffic

Difficulty: ▌▌◊◊◊ **Total distance:** 24.5 miles (or 44.5-mile option)

Riding time: 2 hours   **Elevation gain:** 900 feet

A favorite of Marin County cyclists, this 24.5-mile road ride is an easy-to-moderate loop on mostly level backroads surrounding the small town of Nicasio and its large reservoir. Although these roads see some traffic, especially on nice-weather weekends, most drivers in the area are accustomed to sharing the road with bikes.

The loop begins in Nicasio, a gentrified country town—the kind of place where almost everybody owns at least one horse. If you prefer, you could easily add on up to 10 miles each way by parking near the junction of Lucas Valley Road and U.S. 101, then riding your bike to Nicasio. (To do so, leave your car on one of the side streets that intersects Lucas Valley Road. The road has a wide shoulder for the first four miles, then no shoulder at all for the next six, but not a lot of traffic, either.)

The scenic backroads of the Nicasio Reservoir Loop are favored by Marin County cyclists.

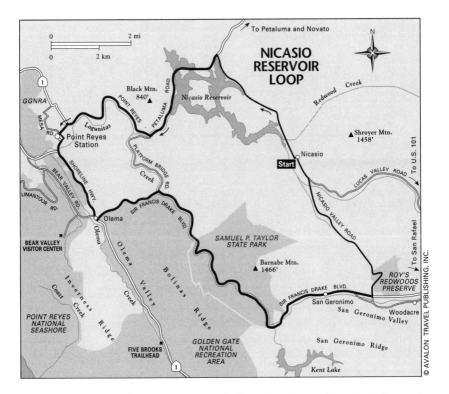

From the town of Nicasio, the loop's first 10 miles on Nicasio Valley Road and Point Reyes-Petaluma Road provide nearly perfect cycling, with a wide shoulder, smooth paved surface, and relatively few cars. The two roads skirt the edge of Nicasio Reservoir, a surprisingly large and pretty lake that is popular year-round for shoreline bass fishing.

Upon reaching Highway 1, you'll ride through Point Reyes Station and Olema—both good stops for coffee, food, and camaraderie with other bikers. Then Sir Francis Drake Boulevard climbs and curves through Samuel P. Taylor State Park and continues gently uphill through a succession of small towns: Lagunitas, Forest Knolls, and San Geronimo. By the golf course in San Geronimo, you'll turn north on Nicasio Valley Road to head back to Nicasio. All in all, this is an easy, low-pressure ride, with plenty of places to stop and enjoy the countryside.

Driving Directions
From San Rafael, drive three miles north on U.S. 101 and take the Lucas Valley Road exit. Drive 10.4 miles west on Lucas Valley Road, then turn right on Nicasio Valley Road. Drive .5 mile and park in the town of Nicasio.

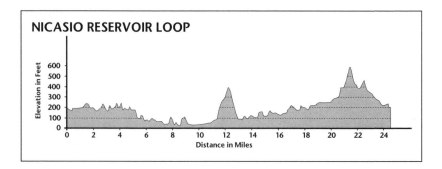

NICASIO RESERVOIR LOOP

Route Directions for Nicasio Reservoir Loop

0.0 Park in the town of Nicasio and ride north on Nicasio Valley Road. *Supplies are available in Nicasio or San Rafael.*

3.2 LEFT on Point Reyes-Petaluma Road.

6.3 RIGHT to stay on Point Reyes-Petaluma Road.

9.4 LEFT on Shoreline Highway (Highway 1).

9.8 LEFT on Shoreline Highway through town of Point Reyes Station. *Supplies are available in town.*

10.0 RIGHT to get back on Highway 1.

10.2 STRAIGHT to stay on Highway 1.

12.2 LEFT on Sir Francis Drake Boulevard in Olema. *Supplies are available in Olema.*

17.0 Pass through Samuel P. Taylor State Park.

20.0 LEFT on Nicasio Valley Road by San Geronimo golf course.

24.5 Arrive at starting point.

10. PINE MOUNTAIN LOOP

Marin Municipal Water District near Fairfax

Type of trail:  dirt road

Difficulty: 🍶🍶🍶🍶🍶

Total distance: 13.2 miles

Riding time: 2.5 hours

Elevation gain: 2,000 feet

The heart and soul of Marin mountain biking lies in the lands west of Fairfax, where the crowded county suburbs give way to grasslands, open ridges, and mixed woodlands of oak, bay, and Douglas fir. The first mile of the Pine Mountain Loop gives you long looks over your right shoulder of the civilization you are leaving behind—much of Marin County, San Pablo Bay, the Richmond Bridge, and Mount Diablo are in plain view—but soon you will see only chaparral-lined hillsides and rolling ridge tops.

The summit of Pine Mountain, elevation 1,762, forms the first challenge in this loop's advanced aerobic workout. You'll climb 700 feet to the top, often on a rutted and rocky surface, in the first 2.3 miles of this loop. The next four miles are much easier; most of your energy will be

A few healthy climbs provide an aerobic workout on the Pine Mountain Loop near Fairfax.

spent controlling your speed on swift descents. A short but lovely section meanders along the edge of Kent Lake. Then at 7.2 miles you'll start to climb again, this time gaining 1,100 feet spaced out over four miles. Gear down and suck in as much oxygen as you can.

An unusual sight worth noting on this route is a stand of dwarf Sargent cypress trees off San Geronimo Ridge Fire Road. The Sargent cypress is a rare evergreen that grows in scattered groves in the region surrounding Mount Tamalpais. It is usually stunted in size when rooted in serpentine soil, as is the case here. Cypress trees that are more than 100 years old may be only a few feet tall. Watch for the miniature Sargent cypress forest between miles 10.5 and 11.

If you are riding in the winter or spring months, you could add a short bike-and-hike adventure to this ride. After the initial 1.1-mile climb on Pine Mountain Road, turn left on Oat Hill Road and ride downhill. Watch for the telephone lines running overhead; at .3 mile from Pine Mountain Road you'll see a single-track trail on the right by a telephone pole with a "No Bikes" sign. Lock up and/or stash your bike, then hike downhill for .3 mile to the top of Carson Falls, one of Marin County's prettiest waterfalls. It's a long chain of four pool-and-drop cataracts that pour into rock-lined pools. Carson Falls's green-grey rock looks like serpentine, but it's actually a type of greenstone basalt.

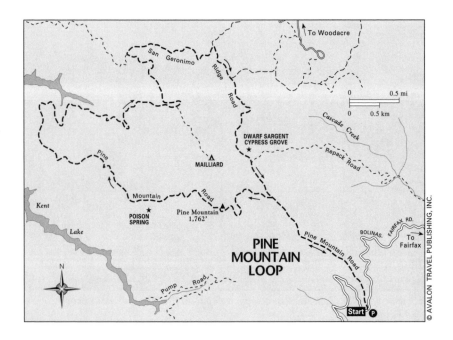

For more information on Marin Municipal Water District lands, phone Sky Oaks Ranger Station at 415/945-1181 or visit www.marinwater.org.

Driving Directions

From San Francisco, cross the Golden Gate Bridge and drive north on U.S. 101 for 7.5 miles. Take the Sir Francis Drake Boulevard exit west toward San Anselmo, then drive six miles to the town of Fairfax. Turn left by the "Fairfax" sign (on Pacheco Road), then turn right immediately on Broadway. In one block, turn left on Bolinas Road. Drive 3.8 miles on Bolinas Road, past the golf course, to the dirt parking area on the left side of the road.

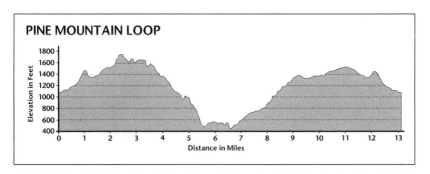

Route Directions for Pine Mountain Loop

0.0 Park in the dirt parking area on the left side of Bolinas-Fairfax Road. The fire road begins across the road. *Supplies are available in Fairfax.*

1.1 STRAIGHT at junction with Oat Hill Road. *Or turn left for the bike-and-hike option to Carson Falls; see route description.*

1.5 LEFT to stay on Pine Mountain Road.

2.3 Summit of Pine Mountain at 1,762 feet.

5.6 RIGHT at junction near Kent Lake.

8.8 RIGHT at four-way intersection.

9.8 RIGHT on San Geronimo Ridge Road.

11.2 RIGHT at junction with Repack Trail (also called Cascade Canyon) on left.11.7 STRAIGHT to rejoin Pine Mountain Road.

12.1 STRAIGHT at junction with Oat Hill Road.

13.2 Arrive at starting point.

11. TAMARANCHO LOOP

Tamarancho Boy Scout Camp near Fairfax

Type of trail: dirt single-track

Difficulty: 𝄔𝄔𝄔𝄔𝄔

Total distance: 10.4 miles

Riding time: 2 hours

Elevation gain: 1,000 feet

It costs 40 bucks to get a permit to ride your mountain bike at the Boy Scouts' Camp Tamarancho (415/454-1081, www.boyscouts-marin.org), but think of it as an annual pass to the best mountain bike park around. Forty dollars will buy you a year's worth of cheap thrills on some gorgeous single-track that was built by mountain bikers for mountain bikers. Or, if you can't stand to part with that much cash, you can buy a $5 one-day pass. Either way, the first time you see the sign that says "Bicycles MUST stay on single-track" you'll think you've died and gone to mountain biking heaven.

Tamarancho is deservedly popular, so the trails can be crowded on weekends. Your best bet is to ride here on a weekday, and preferably not at mid-afternoon in summer, when it can be hot as Hades. There are no trail choices to make, just a single loop set aside for mountain bikers. Yes, it's almost exclusively single-track, and yes again, the loop presents plenty of technical challenges. Beginning riders probably would

You may think you are in mountain biking heaven when you see the signs stating that you must stay on Camp Tamarancho's single-track.

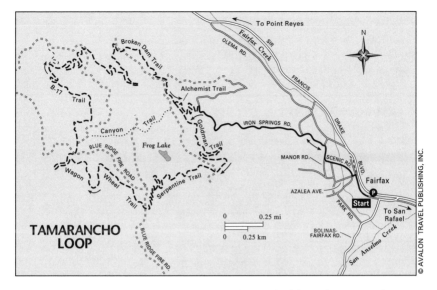

not be happy here. Some hikers also use the trail, although most pedestrians stick to the camp's dirt roads on the inside of this loop, where bikes are not permitted.

The Tamarancho Loop rolls and dips, curving in and out of dense oak and bay woodland and open, grassy areas. Several short climbs of less than a mile in length give you a moderate workout, but without the drudgery of a long, sustained ascent. You'll snake through more than three dozen switchbacks along the route. It's all fun, but make sure your eyes and ears are alert for other riders, because otherwise you won't see them until you're right on top of them.

One leg of the loop, Wagon Wheel Trail, leaves the Boy Scouts' property and travels through Marin County Open Space land. The entire route is well-signed (always watch for the arrow signs where the single-track crosses fire roads). Although the loop itself is about seven miles, the entire ride length is 11.8 miles because there is no parking permitted anywhere near Tamarancho. You leave your car in downtown Fairfax and ride 1.6 miles to a connecting trail off pothole-ridden Iron Springs Road, which deposits you on the loop. The loop itself can be ridden in either direction; a clockwise loop is described below.

Driving Directions

From San Francisco, cross the Golden Gate Bridge and drive north on U.S. 101 for 7.5 miles. Take the Sir Francis Drake Boulevard exit west toward San Anselmo, then drive six miles to the town of Fairfax. Turn left by the

"Fairfax" sign on Pacheco Road, then turn right on Broadway and park in downtown Fairfax. The public parking lot on your right (bordered by Pacheco Road, Sir Francis Drake Boulevard, and Broadway) allows free four-hour parking.

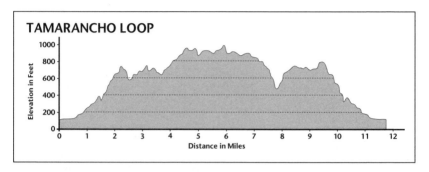

TAMARANCHO LOOP

Route Directions for Tamarancho Loop

0.0 Park in downtown Fairfax in the four-hour parking lot between Sir Francis Drake Boulevard and Broadway. Exit the parking lot and ride west on Broadway. *Supplies are available in downtown Fairfax.*

0.3 LEFT on Azalea (west of Fairfax Lumber), then immediate RIGHT on Scenic.

0.5 RIGHT on Manor.

0.6 LEFT on Rockridge.

0.7 STRAIGHT on Iron Springs Road (Rockridge veers to the right). Watch for large potholes on Iron Springs Road.

1.6 LEFT on single-track connector trail at Tamarancho.

2.0 LEFT on Goldman Trail.

2.9 Cross fire road to join Serpentine Trail.

4.0 Cross fire road to join Wagon Wheel Trail.

5.5 STRAIGHT on fire road to join B-17 Trail on left.

6.4 RIGHT to stay on B-17 Trail.

8.7 Cross fire road to join Goldman Trail.

8.9 LEFT on single-track leading back to Iron Springs Road.

9.4 RIGHT on Iron Springs Road,

11.8 Arrive at starting point.

12. FAIRFAX & MOUNT TAMALPAIS LOOP

Bolinas-Fairfax Road to Mount Tamalpais

Type of trail: paved roads with moderate car traffic

Difficulty: ▮▮▮◌◌

Total distance: 31.8 miles

Riding time: 3–4 hours

Elevation gain: 2,200 feet

If you like country back roads with few cars and a variety of scenic terrain, you'll love riding Bolinas-Fairfax Road. This 32-mile loop travels the rolling upper portion of the old stage road from the town of Fairfax to the top of Bolinas Ridge. (The steeper lower stretch is followed in the Stinson Beach & Mount Tamalpais Loop, Ride 15). The winding pavement curves through miles of open space in the protected lands of the Marin Watershed, where deer and raptors are more common than people, and cyclists are more common than automobiles. Most of the route travels through open grasslands and can be quite warm in the summer months. But the

Ridgecrest Boulevard, with its open views of Mount Tamalpais's grassy slopes and the Pacific coast, is one of the most photographed stretches of road in the San Francisco Bay Area.

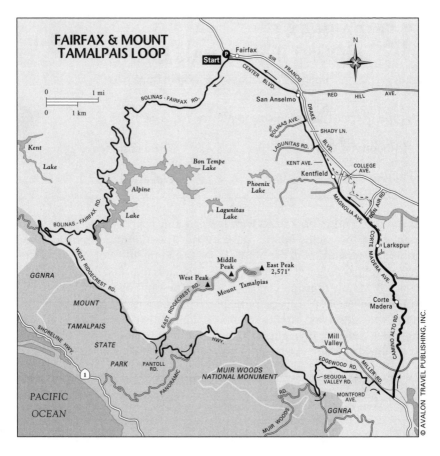

scenery changes dramatically at about seven miles when you reach the western lakeshore of large Alpine Lake, then cross its dam and enter dense redwood forest for a heart-pumping, 2.5-mile climb to Bolinas Ridge (850-foot gain).

At the road's high point, you'll turn left and pedal along one of the Bay Area's most filmed and photographed roads—West Ridgecrest Boulevard, site of dozens of car commercials and calendar shots. Ocean views are dazzling from this high ridge, which is surrounded by the grassy hillsides of Mount Tamalpais State Park. You'll gain another 500 feet as you traverse the ridge, then make a fast descent down Pantoll Road to Panoramic Highway. A left turn here brings you to Four Corners (use caution on this no-shoulder stretch of narrow pavement), where you make a transitional descent from the open ridgeline roads of Mount Tamalpais to the narrow hillside streets of Mill Valley. It's down, down, down for a solid eight miles from the top of Pantoll Road on Mount Tam to Miller Avenue in Mill Valley. Your brakes will get plenty of work.

The final nine miles of the loop are a northward run through the Marin County towns of Corte Madera, Larkspur, Kentfield, Ross, and San Anselmo. A lunch stop at one of the wonderful cafés in downtown Larkspur is highly recommended.

Driving Directions

From San Francisco, cross the Golden Gate Bridge and drive north on U.S. 101 for 7.5 miles. Take the Sir Francis Drake Boulevard exit west toward San Anselmo, then drive six miles to the town of Fairfax. Turn left by the "Fairfax" sign on Pacheco Road, then turn right on Broadway and park in downtown Fairfax. The public parking lot on your right (bordered by Pacheco Road, Sir Francis Drake Boulevard, and Broadway) allows free four-hour parking.

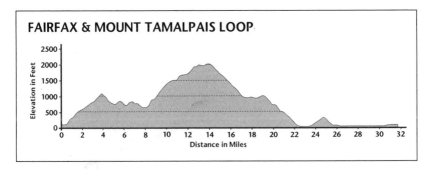

FAIRFAX & MOUNT TAMALPAIS LOOP

Route Directions for Fairfax & Mount Tamalpais Loop

0.0 Park in downtown Fairfax in the four-hour parking lot between Sir Francis Drake Boulevard and Broadway. Exit the parking lot and ride west on Broadway for one block to the start of Bolinas-Fairfax Road. *Supplies are available in downtown Fairfax.*

0.1 LEFT on Bolinas-Fairfax Road (note that this road is sometimes signed as Bolinas Road or Fairfax-Bolinas Road).

7.9 Cross Alpine Dam and begin steep climb through shady redwood forest.

10.4 LEFT on West Ridgecrest Boulevard at top of Bolinas Ridge.

14.3 RIGHT on Pantoll Road; begin fast descent.

15.7 LEFT on Panoramic Highway.

20.2 LEFT on Sequoia Valley Road at Four Corners junction (Sequoia Valley Road changes names to Edgewood Road and then Molino Avenue).

22.0 LEFT on Montford Avenue.

22.1 LEFT to stay on Montford Avenue.

22.3 RIGHT on Miller Avenue. *Supplies are available on Miller Avenue.*

22.7 LEFT on Camino Alto by Tamalpais High School.

23.2 Cross East Blithedale Avenue to stay on Camino Alto; Camino Alto changes names to Corte Madera Avenue and then Magnolia Avenue). *Cafés, restaurants, and supplies are available on Magnolia Avenue in Larkspur.*

26.7 Larkspur bike path runs alongside road; follow path or road.

27.1 Cross Bon Air Road; bike path ends; follow bike lane.

27.9 LEFT on Kent Avenue, which becomes Poplar Avenue.

28.8 LEFT on Lagunitas Road at Ross Commons Park.

28.9 RIGHT on Shady Lane.

29.6 RIGHT on Bolinas Avenue, then immediate LEFT on San Anselmo Avenue.

30.2 Follow Bridge Avenue, then LEFT on Sycamore Avenue (changes names to Center Boulevard, Lansdale Avenue, then back to Center Boulevard).

31.8 Arrive at starting point.

13. CHINA CAMP LOOPS

China Camp State Park near San Rafael
13A (Shoreline Trail Out-and-Back)

Type of trail: dirt single-track

Difficulty: ❚❚❙❙❙ **Total distance:** 11.2 miles (or 8-mile option)

Riding time: 2 hours **Elevation gain:** 250 feet

13B (Ridge Fire Road and Bay View Loop)

Type of trail: dirt road and single-track

Difficulty: ❚❚❚❙❙ **Total distance:** 11.6 miles

Riding time: 2 hours **Elevation gain:** 600 feet

China Camp State Park (415/456-0766 or 415/893-1580) is a rare bird in the California State Park system. One of only a handful of state parks that allows mountain bikes on single-track trails, China Camp also holds a scenic location on San Pablo Bay, with blue-water vistas from more than 1,500 shoreline acres. Bikers and hikers generally mind their manners and get along just fine here, although in recent years the park has seen more

High views of San Pablo Bay and Rat Rock can be seen from China Camp's trails.

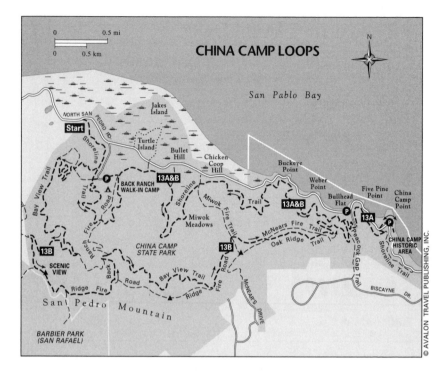

of the former and less of the latter, especially on weekends. China Camp has slowly evolved into a biker's park.

It's also a historic preserve, showcasing the remains of a Chinese shrimp fishing village from the 19th century, where immigrants netted shrimp from the bay. Don't neglect visiting the historic buildings and experiencing the unique history of this area.

Several rides are possible at China Camp. Beginners should stick to the smooth single-track Shoreline Trail (Ride 13A), while more advanced riders will want to tackle the rutted, steep hills in the backcountry of the park (Ride 13B). The latter ride is a good workout and supplies opportunities to practice your uphill and downhill skills—it has plenty of short but steep ones. Highlights include a visit to one of Marin County's best viewpoints, a Nike radar site at 900 feet above the bay; and pedaling on Oak Ridge Trail, a lovely pathway through grasslands and oak woodlands.

Driving Directions

From San Francisco, cross the Golden Gate Bridge and drive north on U.S. 101 for 11 miles to San Rafael. Take the North San Pedro exit and drive east for 3.5 miles to China Camp State Park.

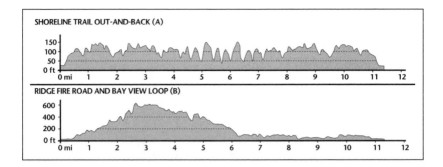

Route Directions for China Camp Loops13A (Shoreline Trail Out-and-Back)

0.0 Park along the road near Back Ranch Meadows Campground. Follow Shoreline Trail from the right side of the kiosk. *Supplies are available in San Rafael, three miles west. Water is available at the campground.*

0.1 LEFT on Shoreline Trail.

0.2 Ride across the parking lot and continue on Shoreline.

2.6 Miwok Meadows Group Camp; follow the dirt road.

2.9 RIGHT on Shoreline Trail.

4.7 LEFT at Y-junction.

4.8 Cross the paved road and continue on trail.

5.2 LEFT on Village Trail.

5.3 Cross San Pedro Road and follow pavement to China Camp Village.

5.6 China Camp Village. TURN AROUND. (If you want to shorten your ride back, return on paved North San Pedro Road instead of Shoreline Trail for an eight-mile loop.) *Lock up your bike and explore the historic buildings and museum. A snack bar is open on weekends and holidays.*

11.2 Arrive at starting point.

Route Directions for 13B (Ridge Fire Road and Bay View Loop)

Follow parking directions for Ride 13A, follow Shoreline Trail from the right side of the kiosk, then continue:

0.1 RIGHT on Bay View Trail.

0.5 RIGHT on fire road, then immediate LEFT back on Bay View Trail.

1.1 LEFT to stay on Bay View Trail.

2.0 RIGHT (hairpin) on trail to Bay Hills Drive.

2.6 LEFT on paved Bay Hills Drive; steep uphill.

3.0 Nike radar base; great views of Marin and San Francisco Bay.

3.3 LEFT on Ridge Fire Road.

3.6 LEFT at junction; steep downhill.

3.9 RIGHT on fire road at power line junction; stay RIGHT on Bay View Trail.

5.2 LEFT at junction with Ridge Fire Road.

5.5 LEFT on Miwok Fire Road for 30 yards, then RIGHT on Oak Ridge Trail.

5.8 Cross fire road to stay on Oak Ridge.

6.2 Cross fire road to stay on Oak Ridge.

6.8 STRAIGHT on Peacock Gap Trail.

6.9 STRAIGHT on Shoreline Trail.

8.7 STRAIGHT on fire road, then RIGHT at restrooms by picnic area to get back on Shoreline Trail.

9.6 LEFT at V-junction.

9.9 LEFT on Shoreline Trail.

10.1 LEFT on Shoreline Trail.

11.6 Arrive at starting point.

14. THREE LAKES LOOP

Marin Municipal Water District near Ross

Type of trail:  dirt road

Difficulty: 🍶🍶🍶🍶🍶

Total distance: 11.2 miles

Riding time: 1.5 hours

Elevation gain: 800 feet

Phoenix Lake is the most popular of the five lakes in the Mount Tamalpais Watershed, but due to a cruel twist of fate it also has the smallest parking lot, with space for only about 15 cars. That means that the hundreds of anglers, hikers, equestrians, baby stroller–pushers, and mountain bikers who want access to Phoenix Lake on summer weekends have to fight it out for a parking space. No street parking is available anywhere near the lake on weekends and holidays (the well-to-do residents of Ross have made sure that their streets are clearly signed and the No Parking rule is strictly enforced), so it's a good thing you're on two wheels. Unless it's a weekday, you must ride a short stretch on the street to gain access to this terrific lake-filled loop.

Lagunitas Lake is the oldest and loveliest of the watershed reservoirs visited on the Three Lakes Loop.

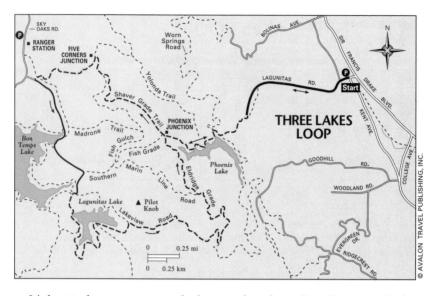

It's best to leave your car at the large parking lot at Ross Commons Park and pedal from there. A 1.1-mile ride brings you to the jam-packed parking lot at Natalie Coffin Greene Park. Go around the gate and uphill to Phoenix Lake's dam. You've arrived at the first lake of the Three Lakes Loop. Ride around the right side of the lake, passing a log cabin built in 1893, then climb uphill on Shaver Grade through dense redwoods to join the paved access road to Bon Tempe and Lagunitas Lakes. After briefly skirting the edge of Bon Tempe Lake, you'll face the best scenery of the day as you circle Lagunitas Lake, crossing three small bridges. Make sure you utilize the bridges and don't take shortcuts across the streams. These waterways are important habitat for newts and other amphimbians. Lagunitas is the oldest of the Marin lakes; its dam was built in 1873. Both Lagunitas and Bon Tempe Lakes are great spots for birdwatching and fishing.

Too soon, you leave the water behind and face a climb up Lakeview Fire Road. Don't forget to turn around and check out the trail's promised "lakeview." The final stretch of the loop follows Eldridge Grade, one of the first wagon routes to the summit of Mount Tamalpais, built in 1889. Be cautious on the steep descent on this old, well-worn trail, which has been reduced to single-track in some stretches.

For more information on Marin Water District lands, phone Sky Oaks Ranger Station at 415/945-1181 or visit www.marinwater.org.

Driving Directions
From San Francisco, cross the Golden Gate Bridge and drive north on U.S.

101 for 7.5 miles. Take the Sir Francis Drake Boulevard exit west toward San Anselmo, then drive three miles to Lagunitas Road on the left, across from the Marin Art and Garden Center. Turn left on Lagunitas Road and park at Ross Commons (junction of Lagunitas and Kent Roads).

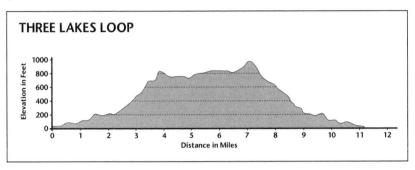

THREE LAKES LOOP

Route Directions for Three Lakes Loop

0.0 Park at Ross Commons. Ride west on Lagunitas Road. *Supplies are available in Ross.*

1.1 Natalie Coffin Greene Park parking lot; go around the gate and across the bridge, climbing up to Phoenix Lake's dam.

1.4 RIGHT to head around the lake.

1.6 LEFT at junction with Worn Springs Road on the right. *Water is available.*

2.0 RIGHT on Shaver Grade at four-way Phoenix Junction.

3.2 LEFT to stay on Shaver Grade at Five Corners Junction.

3.8 LEFT at gate on paved Sky Oaks Road.

4.3 Ride along edge of Bon Tempe Lake on paved road.

5.1 Lake Lagunitas parking lot. Stay on right side of parking lot to pick up the dirt road leading up to the right side of the dam.

5.7 LEFT at junction with Rock Springs/Lagunitas Fire road; stay along the lakeshore.

6.5 RIGHT on Lakeview Fire Road.

7.1 LEFT on Eldridge Grade.

8.4 RIGHT to stay on Eldridge Grade.

9.2 RIGHT at Phoenix Junction; backtrack alongside Phoenix Lake and back to Lagunitas Road.

11.2 Arrive at starting point.

15. STINSON BEACH & MOUNT TAMALPAIS LOOP

Mount Tamalpais State Park

Type of trail:  paved roads with moderate car traffic

Difficulty: 𝐼𝐼𝐼𝐼◊

Total distance: 23.9 miles

Riding time: 3 hours

Elevation gain: 2,700 feet

A day on less-traveled roads showcases the wonders of Mount Tamalpais, from coast to mountaintop. This ride is a workout, but it's worth it.

A level four-mile warm-up alongside Bolinas Lagoon on Highway 1 is followed by a circuitous and unrelenting 1,500-foot climb up the historic Bolinas-Fairfax stage road. When at last you reach the top, prepare yourself for one of the Bay Area's most filmed and photographed roads—West Ridgecrest Boulevard on Mount Tamalpais, site of dozens of car commercials and calendar shots. The trees give way to open grassy hillsides, where deer graze and hang gliders take off for a breezy, graceful descent to the ocean below. You'll keep climbing as you travel the ridge, but much more gradually now.

From the 2,571-foot summit of Mount Tamalpais's East Peak, southern Marin County comes into full view.

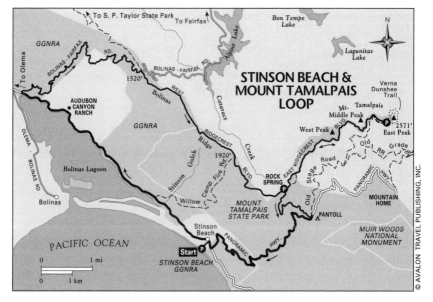

At Rock Springs parking lot and road junction, continue straight for another 2.9 miles to Mount Tamalpais's East Peak at elevation 2,571 feet. The vistas are even better from this summit than what you've seen so far. In addition to the bird's-eye view out to sea, much of Marin County and San Francisco comes into full perspective. East Peak's snack stand is open on weekends to refuel hungry bikers. When you've had your fill of snacks and views, backtrack to the Rock Springs parking lot.

Now it's time for a steep, fast, memorable descent. The traffic will pick up as you drop to Pantoll ranger station, and it will continue racing downhill to the ocean, but you'll be rolling along just as fast, or maybe faster, than the cars. Since you are riding on aptly named Panoramic Highway, take a break now and then to admire the views of the coast ahead and Mount Tamalpais behind.

With a final screech of brakes, you come to a stop sign at Highway 1. A right turn and you're back at your car in less than half a mile. Hope you brought your swimsuit for a dip in the ocean at Stinson Beach, or your wallet for a well-deserved meal at the beachside hamburger stand.

For more information, contact Mount Tamalpais State Park, 415/388-2070.

Driving Directions

From San Francisco, cross the Golden Gate Bridge and drive north on U.S. 101 for four miles. Take the Mill Valley/Stinson Beach/Highway 1 exit and continue straight for one mile to a stoplight at Shoreline Highway

(Highway 1). Turn left on Shoreline Highway and drive 12 miles to Stinson Beach. Turn left at the sign for Stinson Beach parking (Golden Gate National Recreation Area).

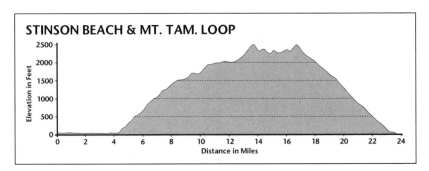

Route Directions for Stinson Beach & Mount Tamalpais Loop

0.0 Park at Stinson Beach parking lot, ride out to Highway 1, and turn left (north). *Supplies are available in town of Stinson Beach.*

1.0 Edge of Bolinas Lagoon; look for hauled-out seals and wide variety of birds.

3.3 Audubon Canyon Ranch. *The ranch, a major great egret nesting site, is open to the public on weekends and holidays from mid-March to mid-July. Walk a .5-mile trail to a viewing platform, then look through sighting scopes into the nests of baby egrets.*

4.3 RIGHT on Bolinas-Fairfax Road (unsigned paved road with open metal gate). Begin 4.4-mile climb.

8.7 RIGHT on West Ridgecrest Boulevard.

12.5 STRAIGHT at Rock Springs parking lot.

15.4 East Peak parking lot; TURN AROUND. *Water and snacks are available. Lock your bike and walk the one-mile Verna Dunshee Trail that circumnavigates the peak.*

18.3 LEFT at Rock Springs parking lot.

19.8 RIGHT on Panoramic Highway at Pantoll junction. *Water is available across the road by the ranger station.*

23.5 RIGHT on Highway 1.

23.9 LEFT into Stinson Beach parking lot; arrive at starting point.

16. OLD STAGE ROAD & OLD RAILROAD GRADE TO EAST PEAK

Mount Tamalpais State Park

Type of trail:  dirt road

Difficulty: ❚❚◊◊◊

Total distance: 8.0 miles

Riding time: 1.5 hours

Elevation gain: 1,100 feet

Take a ride through Mount Tamalpais history on this eight-mile out-and-back ride to the 2,571-foot East Peak of Mount Tam. Although you could just drive your car on paved roads to the summit, this ride on a stretch of the old Mount Tamalpais Scenic Railway is a much more enjoyable way to get there.

The railway, known in the early 1900s as the "Crookedest Railroad in the World," carried passengers through 281 turns and curves up the slopes of Mount Tamalpais. The last two miles of this ride trace the train's exact route to the mountain summit, while the first two miles follow the route used by passengers who rode the stagecoach to Stinson Beach and

The historic Old Stage Road provides views of Angel Island, southern Marin County, and a peek at the San Francisco skyline.

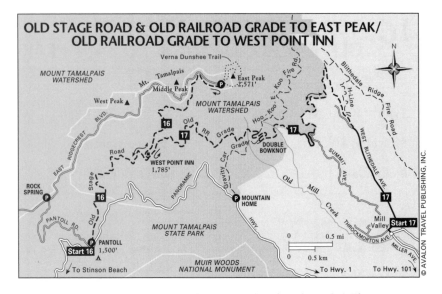

OLD STAGE ROAD & OLD RAILROAD GRADE TO EAST PEAK/ OLD RAILROAD GRADE TO WEST POINT INN

Bolinas. (See Ride 17 for more riding on Old Railroad Grade.) The two halves of this ride converge at West Point Inn, as much a popular stopover for cyclists and hikers today as it was for train and stage passengers 100 years ago.

Begin your ride at the large parking area by Pantoll Ranger Station. After a hasty and cautious crossing of Panoramic Highway, mount your bike and ride on paved Old Stage Road. The pavement soon turns to dirt and the views of San Francisco and Marin start to amaze you. Old Stage Road's grade is remarkably gradual as it winds through myriad twists and turns.

At West Point Inn, fill up your water bottle at an old stone fountain, or buy a glass of lemonade and have a seat on the outside deck, then pick up Old Railroad Grade on the inn's west side and continue uphill to East Peak. This dirt road is steeper, and more rocky, than Old Stage Road. At the trail's end you'll find yourself at the paved East Peak parking lot, enjoying far-reaching views of Marin County, the East Bay, and San Francisco and its bridges. Be sure to walk up the stairs to the Gardner Fire Lookout so you can say you went to the tip-top of the mountain.

If you don't want to ride back the way you came, you can always follow the paved route back to Pantoll: Take Ridgecrest Boulevard 2.9 miles to Rock Spring, then turn left on Pantoll Road and ride 1.5 miles downhill. This is a fun loop if you don't mind some car traffic.

Contact Mount Tamalpais State Park, 415/388-2070, for more information.

Driving Directions

From San Francisco, cross the Golden Gate Bridge and drive north on U.S. 101 for four miles. Take the Mill Valley/Stinson Beach/Highway 1 exit and continue straight for one mile to a stoplight at Shoreline Highway (Highway 1). Turn left on Shoreline Highway and drive 2.5 miles, then turn right on Panoramic Highway. Drive .9 mile to a junction of roads. Continue straight 4.3 miles farther to Pantoll Ranger Station and the parking lot on the left.

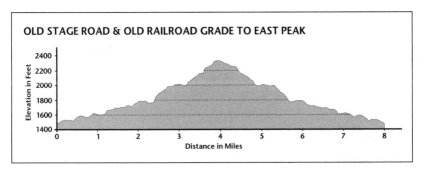

OLD STAGE ROAD & OLD RAILROAD GRADE TO EAST PEAK

Route Directions for Old Stage Road & Old Railroad Grade to East Peak

0.0 Park by Pantoll Ranger Station, then cross Panoramic Highway to the start of Pantoll Road. On the right is a paved road signed "Old Stage Road to East Peak." *Supplies are available in Mill Valley.*

0.1 Begin riding on Old Stage Road.

0.4 Pavement turns to dirt.

2.0 West Point Inn. After enjoying the view, pick up Old Railroad Grade on the left (west) side of the inn. *Water and snacks are available.*

4.0 RIGHT on pavement at East Peak parking lot; TURN AROUND. *A small visitor center, overlook area, and Gardner Lookout are located here. Walk the Verna Dunshee Trail or climb the stairs to the lookout for the best view of the day.*

8.0 Arrive at starting point.

17. OLD RAILROAD GRADE TO WEST POINT INN

Mill Valley to Mount Tamalpais

Type of trail:  dirt road

Difficulty: 𝗜 𝗜 𝗜 𝟬 𝟬   **Total distance:** 13.8 miles (or 17.8-mile option)

Riding time: 2 hours   **Elevation gain:** 1,700 feet

For trail map, see page 64 (Ride 16: Old Stage Road & Old Railroad Grade to East Peak)

Beginning in Mill Valley, this popular ride on the slopes of Mount Tamalpais follows the lower route of the "Crookedest Railroad in the World," a major tourist attraction that carried passengers up the mountain in the early 1900s. Your destination is historic West Point Inn (415/388-9955 or 415/646-0702), built in 1904 to serve railway passengers; it's still serving cyclists and hikers today. The inn has small cabins for rent and sells drinks and snacks (closed on Monday). Its water fountain will come in handy after you ride these 6.7 ascending (and dusty in summer) miles.

Mountain bikers use historic West Point Inn as a rest stop on the ascent up Mount Tamalpais.

Downtown Mill Valley is Cyclist Central on fair-weather weekends. You'll have to park a mile or so from the start of Old Railroad Grade; there is almost no parking at the trailhead. From downtown, follow West Blithedale Road to the Marin Open Space District gate at the start of the railroad grade. This is your level warm-up; soon you start to climb on a remarkably consistent grade. A highlight on the ride is the "double bowknot," where the Crookedest Railroad curved through a series of tight, gradual switchbacks. You'll know it when you ride it.

This is an excellent ride for mountain bikers who have progressed past the beginner stage but aren't interested (or ready for) very technical riding. It is a solid aerobic and leg workout with only minor challenges from rocks and ruts. Note that if you wish to add a few more miles, Old Railroad Grade continues another two miles from West Point Inn to East Peak (see Ride 16). From there, you could retrace your tire treads or loop back on Eldridge Grade, Indian Fire Road, and Hoo Koo E Koo Road. A Mount Tamalpais State Park (415/388-2070) or Marin Municipal Water District (415/945-1195) map gives all the details.

Driving Directions

From San Francisco, cross the Golden Gate Bridge and drive north on U.S. 101 for six miles. Take the Tiburon/Highway 131/East Blithedale Avenue exit, then turn left and drive two miles west on East Blithedale. Turn left on Throckmorton Avenue and drive one block to Miller Avenue in downtown Mill Valley.

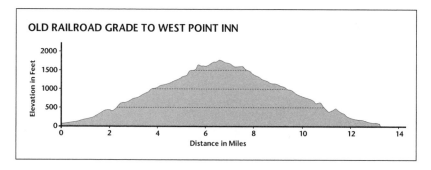

OLD RAILROAD GRADE TO WEST POINT INN

Route Directions for Old Railroad Grade to West Point Inn

0.0 Park near the junction of Miller and Throckmorton Avenues in Mill Valley. Ride north on Throckmorton for one block to its junction with East and West Blithedale Avenues. *Supplies are available in the surrounding blocks.*

0.1 LEFT on West Blithedale.

1.4 RIGHT at gate on dirt Old Railroad Grade.

2.1 LEFT at junction.

3.3 RIGHT on pavement (uphill) where dirt road ends.

3.7 Back on dirt road.

4.4 RIGHT at junction; start of "double bowknot."

6.9 West Point Inn. TURN AROUND or continue 2 miles to East Peak (see route description). *Water and snacks are usually available.*

13.8 Arrive at starting point.

18. TIBURON & BELVEDERE LOOP

Tiburon Peninsula

Type of trail: bike path and paved roads with moderate car traffic

Difficulty: 🍼🍼🍼🍼🍼 **Total distance:** 10.5 miles (or longer options)

Riding time: 1 hour **Elevation gain:** 700 feet

This combined bike path and paved road ride provides the chance to pedal around some prime real estate along scenic San Francisco Bay—the type of property that 99.9 percent of us would never be able to afford in our wildest dreams. For easy riding with stunning bay views, you can't do much better than the Tiburon and Belvedere Loop.

The first part of the ride follows the Tiburon Bike Path from Blackie's Pasture, just outside of the town of Tiburon. The popular trailhead is well known for its large statue of a horse, which was built to commemorate Blackie, who grazed in this pasture until his salad days ended at the ripe old age of 33, in 1966. Local admirers put up a gravestone, and later this handsome statue, in his memory.

Million-dollar views of the Golden Gate Bridge are yours for the taking on the Tiburon & Belvedere Loop.

The bike path travels east for 2.3 miles into downtown Tiburon, although the ride described here leaves the path after the first mile. This converted rail trail was once the track of the Northwestern Pacific Railroad, which provided passenger and freight service from Corte Madera to Tiburon. The trail provides close-up bay views—the water laps within 20 feet of the trail at high tide—and glimpses of Sausalito, the Golden Gate Bridge, and Mount Tamalpais. At low tide, birdwatching is rewarding, as long-legged types are perpetually digging in the mudflats for worms. The trail also passes the Richardson Bay Wildlife Ponds. Managed by the Richardson Bay Sanitary District, these small bird ponds make good use of Tiburon's sewage.

After a right turn on San Rafael Avenue, you'll ride through ultra-wealthy Belvedere neighborhoods and enjoy a free show of multi-million-dollar bay views. The streets narrow to one lane wide; it's a wonder there aren't more collisions between Bentleys and Rolls Royces. Stay as far to the right as you can. Next you'll drop into downtown Tiburon, which is usually packed with tourists on weekends. Hang out with the crowds and

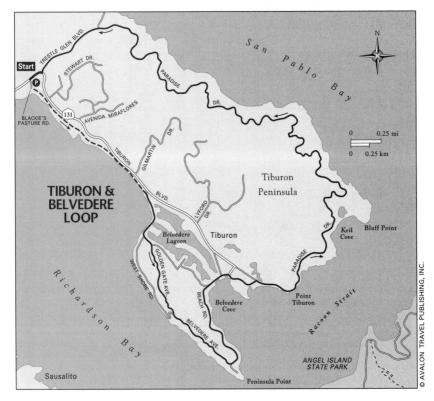

explore the shops, or make a quick escape by turning right on Paradise Drive and climbing your first serious hill, which lasts for nearly a half mile. You'll stay on well-named Paradise Drive for most of the rest of this ride. Although the road is extremely narrow and has virtually no shoulder, traffic is generally light and cars must drive slowly because of its multiple winding curves. As you wind northward, the houses eventually become fewer and farther in between and views of north San Pablo Bay open wide. You'll pass the entrance to Paradise Beach Park, a popular hangout on summer weekends. People come from all over Marin County for swimming and sunning here.

Too soon, you reach a junction with Trestle Glen Drive and must turn back to Blackie's Pasture. But there are multiple options for extending the ride. Many cyclists start in Mill Valley or Sausalito and ride to Blackie's instead of driving there (most of the route can be traveled on bike paths). Some riders begin their trip in San Francisco, follow the Sausalito and Mill Valley bike paths to Tiburon, cruise around this loop, have lunch at a local restaurant, then take the easy way home—by riding the ferry back to San Francisco. Those who are more ambitious simply ride back. No matter how you do it, it's a fine way to spend a day.

Driving Directions

From San Francisco, cross the Golden Gate Bridge and drive north on U.S. 101 for six miles. Take the Tiburon/Highway 131/East Blithedale Avenue exit and drive east for 1.5 miles, then turn right at Blackie's Pasture Road and park in the large parking lot.

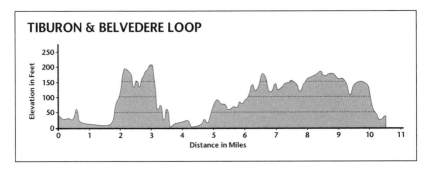

Route Directions for Tiburon & Belvedere Loop

0.0 Park at Blackie's Pasture parking lot. Ride east on the paved bike trail. *Supplies are available in Mill Valley or Tiburon.*

1.2 RIGHT on San Rafael Avenue (leave bike path).

1.6 LEFT to stay on San Rafael Avenue.

1.7 RIGHT on Golden Gate Avenue and up the hill.

1.9 STRAIGHT at stop sign.

2.0 Cross intersection and continue on Belvedere Avenue (straight and slightly to the right).

3.2 RIGHT on Beach Road.

3.5 RIGHT to stay on Beach Road.

3.8 STRAIGHT at stop sign (stay on Beach Road).

4.0 RIGHT on Main Street. *Supplies are available in downtown Tiburon.*

4.3 RIGHT on Paradise Drive.

6.6 Trailhead for Tiburon Uplands Nature Preserve on left (hiking trail only).

7.6 Paradise Beach Park on right. *Water is available.*

9.7 LEFT on Trestle Glen Drive.

10.2 Cross Tiburon Boulevard at stoplight and crosswalk; pick up bike path on far side and ride west (to your right).

10.4 LEFT into Blackie's Pasture parking lot.

10.5 Arrive at starting point.

19. TENNESSEE VALLEY & COYOTE RIDGE

Golden Gate National Recreation Area near Mill Valley

19A (Tennessee Valley Trail to Beach)

Type of trail: dirt road

Difficulty: ❚ ⭕⭕⭕⭕

Riding time: 1 hour

Total distance: 3.8 miles

Elevation gain: 250 feet

19B (Tennessee Valley & Coyote Ridge Loop)

Type of trail: dirt road and single-track

Difficulty: ❚❚❚ ⭕⭕

Riding time: 1.5 hours

Total distance: 5.3 miles

Elevation gain: 1,200 feet

On weekends, the Tennessee Valley Trailhead in Mill Valley is busier than a shopping mall at Christmas. The parking lot is filled with a mix of bikers, walkers, and runners, all wanting to get a piece of the scenery at Tennessee Valley Beach and/or its surrounding ridges and hillsides.

Lock up your bike, take off your cycling shoes, and explore the black sands of Tennessee Valley Beach.

And no wonder; there's something for everyone here. Biking families and novice riders enjoy the easy, wide dirt road that rolls gently out to Tennessee Beach, a black gravel pocket beach framed by jagged bluffs on both sides. Mountain bikers seeking more of a challenge choose from two possible loops: Tennessee Valley and Coyote Ridge to the west, or Miwok and Bobcat to the east. (The latter loop can also be accessed from the Marin Headlands and is described in Ride 20.)

Those simply following Tennessee Valley Trail to the beach (Ride 19A) will find the path amazingly easy and scenic. Bring a picnic and a bike lock (a bike rack is provided) for the picturesque beach, and be sure to hike up the short trail on the north bluff for a memorable view of the coast.

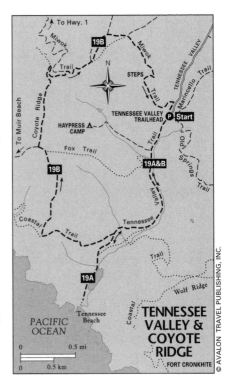

Those following the Tennessee Valley and Coyote Ridge Loop (Ride 19B) will cut off .5 mile before the beach (or go check it out first while you're here), then make a short but hellacious climb up Coastal Trail. At the summit, catch your breath and enjoy the views, because there's more climbing ahead on Coyote Ridge Trail. A final downhill stint on Miwok Trail will bring you back to Tennessee Valley Trailhead with some exciting—and surprisingly technical—single-track. (Don't let the railroad-tie stairs .5 mile from the end catch you by surprise.) This loop's total mileage is short, but the steep uphills and rutted dirt trails dole out a solid workout. Oh yeah, and the Marin Headlands scenery never disappoints.

For further information, call Golden Gate National Recreation Area, 415/331-1540, or visit www.nps.gov/goga.

Driving Directions

From San Francisco, cross the Golden Gate Bridge and drive north on U.S. 101 for four miles. Take the Mill Valley/Stinson Beach/Highway 1 exit and continue straight for .6 mile to Tennessee Valley Road on the left. Turn left and drive two miles to the trailhead.

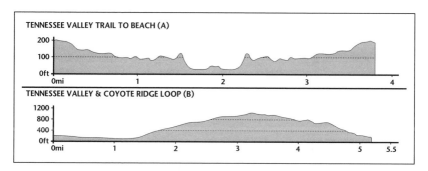

Route Directions for Tennessee Valley & Coyote Ridge 19A (Tennessee Valley Trail to Beach)

0.0 Park at Tennessee Valley Trailhead and follow the main, wide road southwest. *Supplies are available in Mill Valley, two miles north.*

1.3 STRAIGHT at junction with Coastal Trail.

1.9 Tennessee Beach bike rack. TURN AROUND.

3.8 Arrive at starting point.

Route Directions for 19B (Tennessee Valley & Coyote Ridge Loop)

Follow directions for Ride 19A to the 1.3-mile mark, then continue:

1.3 RIGHT at junction with Coastal Trail; hill climb.

1.9 RIGHT at junction.

2.6 LEFT then immediate RIGHT on Coyote Ridge Trail.

3.1 STRAIGHT at two Green Gulch junctions.

3.2 High point and end of climb.

3.4 STRAIGHT on Miwok Trail.

4.2 RIGHT to stay on Miwok Trail.

4.4 STRAIGHT on Miwok at junction with Countryview Road Trail on left.

5.3 Arrive at starting point.

20. MARIN HEADLANDS MIWOK & BOBCAT LOOP

Golden Gate National Recreation Area near Sausalito

Type of trail: dirt road and single-track; paved roads with moderate car traffic

Difficulty: 𝌆𝌆𝌆𝌆𝌆

Total distance: 14 miles

Riding time: 2 hours

Elevation gain: 2,100 feet

Riders can choose from many possible starting points for this loop: the San Francisco or Marin sides of the Golden Gate Bridge, the Tennessee Valley Trailhead in Mill Valley, the Rodeo Avenue exit off U.S. 101 near Sausalito, or Rodeo Beach at the Marin Headlands. I describe starting from the Conzelman parking lot on the northwest side of the Golden Gate Bridge because that allows for the most off-road miles. (Three of the total 14 miles are paved; the rest are wide fire roads and single-track.) Ride this loop any way you like; it's all good.

Like the other Marin Headlands loop described in this book (Ride 19B),

The long climb on Miwok Trail to the top of Wolf Ridge in the Marin Headlands will get your heart and lungs pumping.

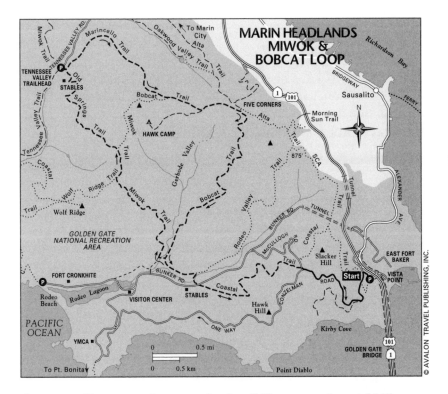

this route offers ocean views, grasslands, wildflowers, and coastal hills. Two significant climbs will get your heart and lungs pumping. One is a 1.5-mile stretch on Miwok Trail from Rodeo Valley up to the top of Wolf Ridge. The other is the 1.5-mile Marincello Trail heading uphill from Tennessee Valley. At least they are memorable: You'll gain some wide bluewater views.

A highlight is Bobcat Trail, which drops through one of the Bay Area's most special places, the Gerbode Valley. This beautiful valley was just barely saved from development in the 1960s, when a community for 20,000 people was planned for construction there. With your first glimpse of Gerbode Valley, you'll grimace at the idea of developers paving over its pristine grasslands. Chalk up a victory for the hawks, bobcats, and butterflies.

A backpacking camp is found .5 mile off Bobcat Trail; you could turn this ride into an overnight if you wish. Don't overload your mountain bike's panniers, however, or these Headlands hills will be very unforgiving.

For more information, call Golden Gate National Recreation Area, 415/331-1540, or visit www.nps.gov/goga.

Driving Directions

From San Francisco, cross the Golden Gate Bridge on U.S. 101 and take the first exit north of the bridge, Alexander Avenue. Turn left and loop back under the freeway, then turn right on Conzelman Road (signed for Marin Headlands). Park in the lot on the left, 100 feet up the road.

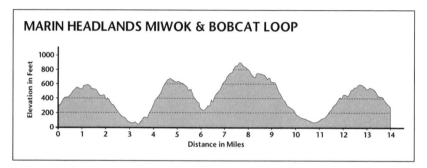

MARIN HEADLANDS MIWOK & BOBCAT LOOP

Route Directions for Marin Headlands Miwok & Bobcat Loop

0.0 Park at lot at start of Conzelman Road, on the northwest side of the Golden Gate Bridge. Ride out of the parking lot and turn left and uphill on Conzelman. *Supplies are available in Sausalito, two miles away.*

1.3 RIGHT at junction with McCullough Road (paved); then LEFT on signed dirt Coastal Trail.

2.9 STRAIGHT at junction to cross paved Bunker Road.

3.0 LEFT on Rodeo Valley Trail.

3.4 LEFT on Bobcat Trail at Y-junction.

3.5 RIGHT on Miwok Trail; now you're on the loop; steep climb ahead.

4.6 RIGHT to stay on Miwok at junction with Wolf Ridge Trail.

4.9 LEFT on Old Springs Trail (single-track).

6.2 Stables at Tennessee Valley Trailhead. Walk your bike through stables and parking lot and pick up Marincello Trail on right (northeast) edge of lot; prepare to climb.

7.7 LEFT on Bobcat Trail.

8.5 RIGHT to stay on Bobcat at junction with Rodeo and Alta Trails; steep descent into Gerbode Valley begins.

10.5 LEFT on Rodeo Valley Trail at end of loop; backtrack on Rodeo Valley Trail, Coastal Trail, and Conzelman Road to parking lot.

14.0 Arrive at starting point.

21. PERIMETER TRAIL & FIRE ROAD LOOPS

Angel Island State Park
21A (Perimeter Trail Only)

Type of trail:  dirt road and deteriorating pavement

Difficulty: 𝆏𝆏𝆏𝆏

Total distance: 5.5 miles

Riding time: 1 hour

Elevation gain: 600 feet

21B (Double Loop)

Type of trail: dirt road and deteriorating pavement

Difficulty: 𝆏𝆏𝆏𝆏𝆏

Total distance: 9.6 miles

Riding time: 2 hours

Elevation gain: 900 feet

The Perimeter Trail at Angel Island State Park provides 360-degree views from its setting in the middle of the bay, making it arguably the most scenic bike trail in the entire Bay Area. Views change constantly as you pedal, allowing you to see the cities and towns surrounding the bay in an entirely new perspective. One of the best vistas lies on the southeast side of the

A bench with a view of the Golden Gate Bridge on Angel Island's Perimeter Trail.

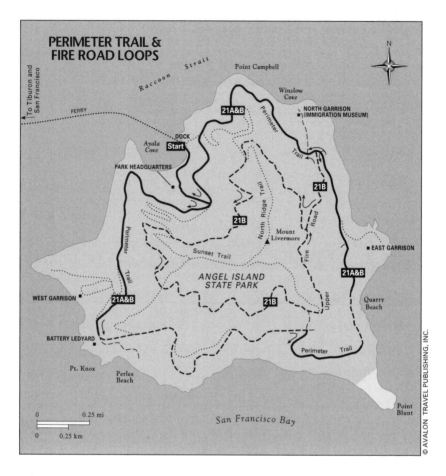

island, where an open stretch captures the Bay and Golden Gate Bridges, plus Alcatraz Island. The 180-degree scene encompasses the whole sweep of urban skylines from Berkeley to San Francisco to Sausalito.

And the island doles out more than just views. Bikers on the Perimeter Trail can also enjoy two sandy beaches just off the trail, a series of history lessons, and the simple joy of getting to the island—a half-hour ferry cruise from various cities around the Bay.

Perimeter Trail is a partially paved road, with the pavement deteriorating to gravel and dirt in places. True to its name, the trail loops around the island's perimeter, so you can ride your bike in either direction (the route suggested here goes counterclockwise). History lessons are readily available because Angel Island has had a long and varied history as a military outpost, a Russian sea otter hunters' site, and an immigrant detention center. Be sure to read the interpretive signs around the island or stop in at the visitor center near Ayala Cove to get more information.

Those seeking a longer ride than the 5.5-mile Perimeter Trail can connect to a loop-within-the-loop, a dirt fire road on the island's interior (Ride 21B). The route suggested here connects the two loops at the fire station on the north side of the island, but you can also connect them via the cutoff for Mount Livermore on the southeast side. Because the upper fire road is situated higher in elevation, it offers even more expansive views than Perimeter Trail.

One note of caution: The wind can blow at Angel Island, and the fog can come in on a moment's notice, so come prepared with an extra jacket, even on sunny days.

For more information, contact Angel Island State Park, 415/435-1915 or 415/893-1580, website: www.angelisland.org.

Driving Directions
Ferry service to Angel Island is available from Tiburon, San Francisco, Oakland/Alameda, and Vallejo. For Tiburon departures, phone the Tiburon Ferry at 415/435-2131. For Oakland or Alameda departures, phone East Bay Ferry at 510/522-3300. For San Francisco departures, phone Blue & Gold Fleet at 415/773-1188. For Vallejo departures, phone Baylink at 707/64-FERRY (707/643-3779).

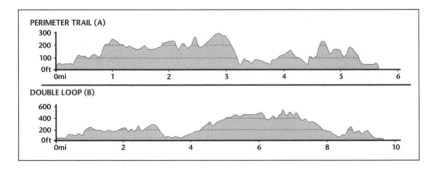

Route Directions for Perimeter Trail & Fire Road Loops 21A (Perimeter Trail Only)

0.0 Arrive at ferry landing at Ayala Cove. Retrieve your bike from the ferry and ride to your right, past the café and toward the picnic area. *Water, pay phones, restrooms, and rental lockers are available at the ferry landing; food is available at the landing café.*

0.2 LEFT on gravel bike trail by picnic area.

0.5 RIGHT on Perimeter Trail.

1.3 West Garrison and Camp Reynolds.

1.7 Cutoff for road to Perle's Beach; views of San Francisco and Alcatraz from the beach.

2.9 STRAIGHT on Perimeter Trail at junction with Upper Fire Road.

3.5 East Garrison and old military hospital.

3.9 STRAIGHT at junction with Upper Fire Road.

5.0 RIGHT at junction with trail to Ayala Cove.

5.5 Arrive at starting point.

Route Directions for 21B (Double Loop)

Follow directions for Ride 21A to the 3.9-mile mark, then continue:

3.9 LEFT at junction with upper Fire Road at Fire Station.

4.3 RIGHT on Fire Road.

7.7 RIGHT on connecting road back to Perimeter Trail.

8.0 LEFT on Perimeter Trail.

9.1 RIGHT at junction with trail to Ayala Cove.

9.6 Arrive at starting point.

22. GOLDEN GATE BRIDGE & MARIN HEADLANDS LOOP

Golden Gate National Recreation Area near Sausalito

Type of trail:  paved roads with moderate car traffic

Difficulty: ▮▮▮▯▯

Total distance: 15 miles

Riding time: 1.5–2 hours

Elevation gain: 1500 feet

This ride is classic San Francisco, with vista after vista of world-class scenery. A favorite training ride for city riders, it's also perfect for visiting tourists seeking a "real" taste of the City by the Bay and its environs.

Beginning at Fort Point in San Francisco's Presidio, the route crosses the Golden Gate Bridge, then follows Conzelman Road through the Marin Headlands, with frequent jaw-dropping views back toward the mouth of the Golden Gate. A challenging climb up to Hawk Hill (920 feet) is followed by a dizzying descent on cliffside Conzelman Road, which thankfully is one-way in this stretch. Make sure your brakes are working well before you begin the precipitous drop.

© ANN MARIE BROWN

Rodeo Beach is an excellent stop for a rest on the Golden Gate Bridge & Marin Headlands Loop.

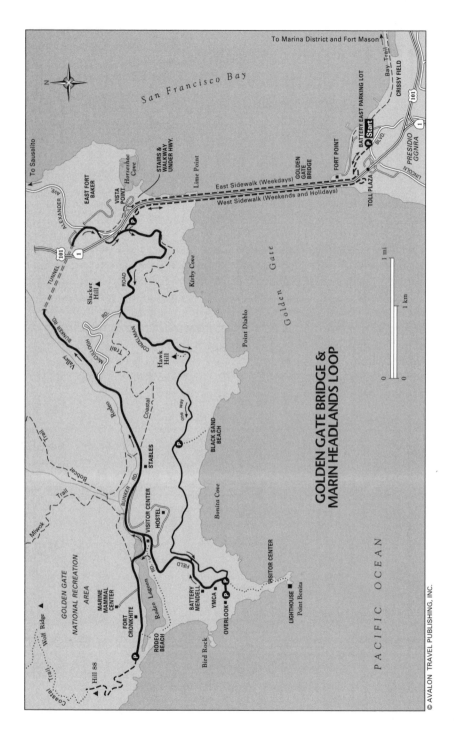

GOLDEN GATE BRIDGE & MARIN HEADLANDS LOOP

At the edge of the headlands, a narrow strip of land curves out to Point Bonita Lighthouse, which can be visited via a one-mile round-trip walk. Time your trip carefully: The 1855-built lighthouse is open only on Saturday, Sunday, and Monday from 12:30 to 3:30 P.M., and is accessed via a 50-foot-long tunnel and 40-yard-long suspension footbridge. Its location is the most dramatic of any lighthouse on the California coast; don't miss seeing it.

Other highlights along the loop include Black Sand Beach, the Marin Headlands Visitor Center, and beautiful Rodeo Beach and Rodeo Lagoon. With all these places to visit, a bike lock is more than a good idea. The trip back includes a ride through a long, lighted tunnel with bike lanes, and then another jaunt across the magnificent Golden Gate Bridge.

Use some caution in crossing the bridge, especially if you ride on a weekday when you must use the east sidewalk (shared with oblivious pedestrians toting video cameras). On weekends, cyclists ride on the west sidewalk while pedestrians use the east sidewalk, so there's less congestion. Either way, keep your speed down and take time to enjoy the view from 225 feet above San Francisco Bay.

For more information, contact Golden Gate National Recreation Area, 415/331-1540, website: nps.gov/goga.

Driving Directions

From the Crissy Field and marina area of San Francisco, take Lincoln Boulevard west toward the Golden Gate Bridge. Turn right just before the bridge entrance into the Battery East parking lot at Fort Point.

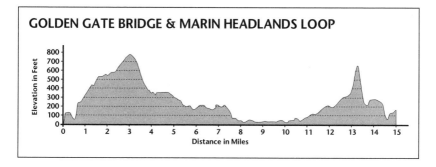

Route Directions for Golden Gate Bridge & Marin Headlands Loop

0.0 Park at the Battery East parking lot at Fort Point on Lincoln Boulevard (east side of the Golden Gate Bridge). At the entrance to the parking lot is a gated, paved road that is signed as a bike route (#202) to get on the bridge. *Water and snacks are available at Bridge Cafe at the bridge entrance (Bridge View Area).*

0.2 Start across the Golden Gate Bridge (ride on west side on weekends and holidays and east side on weekdays; obey all posted instruction signs for cyclists).

1.8 LEFT up hill on Conzelman Road at north (Marin County) side of Golden Gate Bridge. *If you're on the east sidewalk, exit at the Vista Point area and take the stairway underpass under the highway to the start of Conzelman Road. If you're on the west sidewalk, follow the signs for cyclists to the start of Conzelman Road.*

3.5 LEFT at junction with McCullough Road.

4.1 Summit of Hawk Hill; two-way road turns to one-way and descent begins.

5.0 Parking lot for Black Sand Beach on left. *Lock up your bike and hike .5 mile to one of Marin County's most spectacular beaches.*

6.0 STRAIGHT for Point Bonita Lighthouse.

6.5 Lighthouse trailhead. *Lock up your bike and hike .5 mile to the lighthouse.*

6.7 Road ends at Battery Mendell and overlook. TURN AROUND.

7.8 Marin Headlands Visitor Center on left.

8.0 LEFT at junction with Bunker Road.

8.5 LEFT at junction; Marin Mammal Center above to the right.

8.9 Road ends at Rodeo Beach parking lot. TURN AROUND. *Lock up your bike and explore the beach and lagoon trail. Mountain bikers can continue up Coastal Trail (gated road) 1.6 miles from parking lot to top of Hill 88 and spectacular view; a turnaround is required at the top.*

10.0 LEFT at junction of Field Road and Bunker Road.

12.2 Entrance to one-way tunnel. Push button to alert motorists that a cyclist is in the tunnel.

12.7 Exit tunnel and ride uphill.

12.9 RIGHT at stop sign.

13.2 Start of Conzelman Road. Return to proper side of the bridge according to day of the week.

15.0 Arrive at starting point.

© ANN MARIE BROWN

Chapter 2

East Bay

23. NIMITZ WAY & WILDCAT CANYON

Tilden and Wildcat Canyon Regional Parks, Berkeley hills

23A (Nimitz Way Trail Only)

Type of trail: paved bike path

Difficulty: 𝘐 🍶🍶🍶🍶

Total distance: 7.8 miles

Riding time: 1 hour

Elevation gain: 450 feet

23B (Nimitz Way & Wildcat Canyon Loop)

Type of trail: dirt road and paved bike path

Difficulty: 𝘐𝘐 🍶🍶🍶

Total distance: 11.3 miles

Riding time: 2 hours

Elevation gain: 800 feet

Of all the paved recreation trails in the East Bay, Nimitz Way wins the prize for best views. Perched on the tip of San Pablo Ridge in Tilden Park, the trail serves up nonstop scenery changes. Near its start, cyclists survey San Pablo Reservoir, with Briones Reservoir behind, plus looming Mount

In contrast to the high ridgeline ride on Nimitz Way, Wildcat Creek Trail rolls along the base of Wildcat Canyon, paralleling its stream.

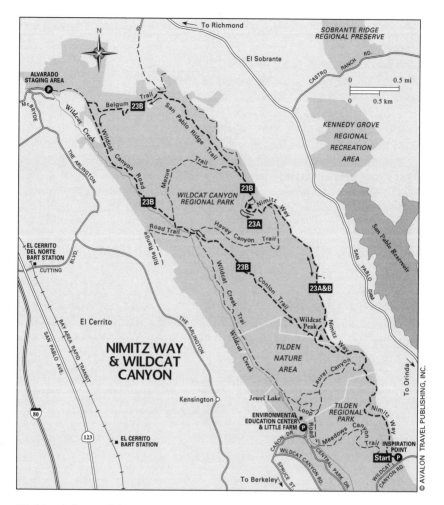

Diablo. A few pedal cranks later, San Francisco Bay, the Golden Gate Bridge, and Angel Island come into view. At every turn in the trail, over every hill, you gain a different perspective: The Richmond Bridge appears, the Gold Coast shows up, San Francisco's skyline emerges, and the Brothers Islands steal the scene. On a clear day, the panorama will amaze you.

Nimitz Way is mostly level with only one short hill right before the pavement ends at 3.9 miles. It is well loved by every kind of rider, including those on tricycles and training wheels, and with good reason. Mountain bikers can use Nimitz Way to connect to dirt trails in Tilden and Wildcat Canyon parks; Ride 23B describes an easy-to-moderate loop through Wildcat that affords a good workout and more memorable views.

Be forewarned that the loop has two very steep downhills, where I've seen riders walking their bikes while simultaneously biting their nails. Hey, at least you don't have to ride *up* those hills.

If you're planning on riding in this area on the weekend, get to the Inspiration Point parking lot early. The place is Bike City every Saturday and Sunday, and parking spots are at a premium.

For more information, contact East Bay Regional Park District, 510/562-7275 or 510/635-0135, website: www.ebparks.org.

Driving Directions
From I-580 in Oakland, take Highway 24 east. Go through the Caldecott Tunnel and exit at Orinda. Turn left on Camino Pablo. Drive north for two miles, then turn left on Wildcat Canyon Road. Drive 2.4 miles to the Inspiration Point parking lot.

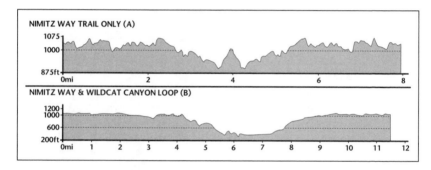

Route Directions for 23A (Nimitz Way Trail Only)

0.0 Park at Inspiration Point parking lot and take the well-signed Nimitz Way Trail. *Supplies are available in Berkeley or Orinda.*

3.9 End of paved Nimitz Way Trail at gate. TURN AROUND.

7.8 Arrive at starting point.

Route Directions for 23B (Nimitz Way & Wildcat Canyon Loop)

Follow the route directions for 23A to mile 3.9, then continue:

3.9 Go through gate at end of Nimitz Way to join dirt San Pablo Ridge Trail; ignore trails branching right and left.

5.2 LEFT on Belgum Trail; steep descent.

6.1 LEFT on Wildcat Creek Trail. *Water is available .5 mile to the right on Wildcat Creek Trail (Alvarado Staging Area).*

7.7 STRAIGHT at junction with Mezue Trail on left.

7.9 LEFT at junction with Havey Canyon Trail then immediate RIGHT on Conlon Trail.

9.9 RIGHT on paved Nimitz Way.

11.3 Arrive at starting point.

24. SKYLINE LOOP

Berkeley and Oakland hills

Type of trail:  paved roads with moderate car traffic

Difficulty: ▌▌▌▐▐ **Total distance:** 28.5 miles (or 23-mile option)

Riding time: 2 hours   **Elevation gain:** 2,000 feet

You can't call yourself a road cyclist in the San Francisco Bay Area until you've ridden the Skyline Loop in the East Bay hills. On a clear day, the loop's far-reaching views of San Francisco Bay, the cities of the East Bay, and Mount Diablo will knock your socks off. The route has just enough hills to provide a workout, but none are so steep that they are out of the range of possibility for most riders. Plus, the roads have surprisingly little traffic, except for Moraga Way, which has a wide shoulder. All this and you can easily start the ride from Orinda, Moraga, Berkeley, or at one of several parks on Skyline Boulevard.

I describe the loop starting from the Inspiration Point parking lot at Tilden Regional Park, a popular gathering place for cyclists on weekends

Far-reaching views of San Francisco Bay and the East Bay cities are seen from the Skyline Loop.

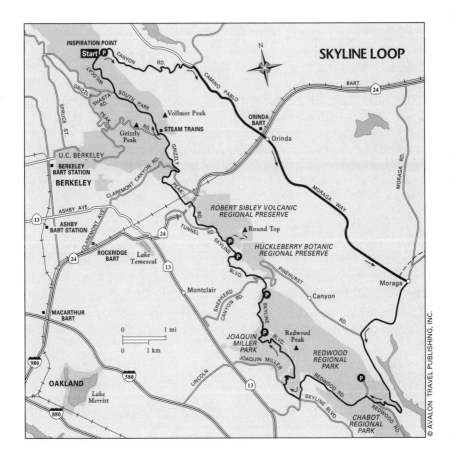

and a great place to find a riding partner. (Get there early to procure a parking spot.) This trailhead choice means you begin your ride with a twisty descent and end with a twisty climb on Wildcat Canyon Road. But the ride has a multitude of climbs and descents, so you might as well get in the spirit right away.

The major hills are on Pinehurst Road, Skyline Boulevard, and Grizzly Peak Road. (The latter two roads are where you gain most of your bay views.) You also face a steep descent on South Park Drive, just after you pass the miniature steam train at Tilden Park, where families pay a couple bucks to go for a 12-minute, open-air train tour. Keep your speed down as you descend on this moderately busy park road. Not just to avoid cars, but also to avoid California newts: The cute brown and orange salamanders cross the road by the thousands each year during the rainy season. During the peak newt migration, South Park Drive is closed to cars, but open to cyclists.

Besides Tilden, this loop passes by two other East Bay Regional Parks: Redwood Regional and Robert Sibley. Redwood is a popular spot for mountain biking and hiking; Sibley has Round Top Peak, the remains of an ancient volcano.

For riders short on time, note the shortcut at mile 10.9 on Pinehurst Road. Turning right instead of left on Pinehurst will cut 5.5 miles off the loop, but you'll face a steep climb up to Skyline Boulevard. The Pinehurst shortcut does have charms, however: The road sees almost no car traffic, is lined with redwoods, and passes by the tiny hamlet of Canyon, with its one-room schoolhouse and post office. You may ask yourself, is this the East Bay?

Driving Directions

From I-580 in Oakland, take Highway 24 east. Go through the Caldecott Tunnel and exit at Orinda. Turn left on Camino Pablo. Drive north for two miles, then turn left on Wildcat Canyon Road. Drive 2.4 miles to Inspiration Point parking lot.

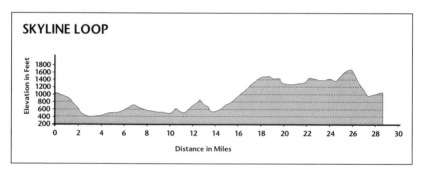

Route Directions for Skyline Loop

0.0 Park at Inspiration Point parking lot. Turn left out of the lot and head downhill on Wildcat Canyon Road. *Supplies are available in Berkeley or Orinda.*

2.4 RIGHT on Camino Pablo Road.

4.5 Cross under Highway 24; Camino Pablo becomes Moraga Way.

4.6 Arrive in Orinda. *Supplies are available.*

9.1 RIGHT on Canyon Road. *Supplies are available at the shopping center.*

10.9 LEFT on Pinehurst Road. *You can cut 5.5 miles off the loop by turning right on Pinehurst Road here. After a steep climb, you'll rejoin the route at mile 20.4, below, where you'll go straight onto Skyline.*

13.8 RIGHT on Redwood Road.

16.2 RIGHT on Skyline Boulevard.

16.8 RIGHT to stay on Skyline Boulevard at Joaquin Miller Road.

19.9 Redwood Regional Park Skyline gate. *Water is available.*

20.4 LEFT to stay on Skyline Boulevard at Pinehurst Road.

21.9 Robert Sibley Regional Preserve. *Water is available.*

22.0 RIGHT on Grizzly Peak Road.

24.4 STRAIGHT to stay on Grizzly Peak Road.

25.6 Tilden Regional Park's miniature steam train. *Water is available.*

25.8 RIGHT on South Park Road.

27.3 RIGHT on Wildcat Canyon Road.

28.5 Arrive at starting point.

25. CARQUINEZ STRAIT LOOP

Martinez to Crockett

Type of trail:  paved roads with minimal car traffic

Difficulty: ❚❚❏❏❏

Total distance: 18.5 miles

Riding time: 1.5–2 hours

Elevation gain: 1,200 feet

The northeastern arm of the conglomeration of waterways that constitute the bay and river delta, Carquinez Strait forms the narrow passageway between San Pablo and Suisun Bays. It's the meeting place of the Sacramento and San Joaquin Rivers, where they join together to flow to the Pacific Ocean through the Golden Gate.

Hundreds of thousands of king salmon once passed through here on their way to the Sacramento and San Joaquin Rivers to spawn. Native Americans lived off their abundance for centuries. In the 1800s, white settlers set up commercial fishing operations and canneries along the strait; king salmon ruled the economy of this area. Today, the only salmon you'll find in the towns of Martinez and Crockett are on dinner plates in

Grasses and weeds push up through the broken pavement on this stretch of Carquinez Scenic Drive, which has been closed to cars since 1982.

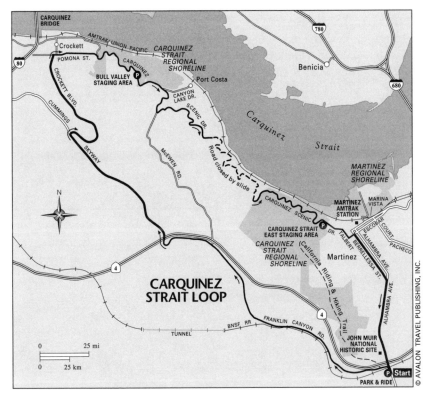

the nicer restaurants, but it's fascinating to recall the area's history as you ride this road tour between the two towns.

Due to events in more recent history, one portion of this road loop is closed to cars. A landslide in 1982 washed out a 1.7-mile-long section of Carquinez Scenic Drive. There's still enough road left for cyclists, but watch for broken pavement, gravel, and rocks. It's easy to get distracted by the views overlooking Carquinez Strait, a wide expanse of blue waterway punctuated by the journeying of ships, large and small. As Carquinez Scenic Drive twists and turns, you gain changing views of the Carquinez Bridge and the towns of Benecia and Vallejo.

Most of the climbing is accomplished in the first five miles of this ride (600-foot gain). The rest of the loop's "ups" are short, 200-foot-or-less climbs. There's also an exhilarating downhill on Crockett Boulevard into Crockett.

For more views of the waterway, you might want to stop at Carquinez Strait Regional Shoreline just outside of Crockett and hike the one-mile Carquinez Overlook Loop Trail.

Driving Directions

From Walnut Creek, take I-680 north for six miles to Highway 4. Turn west on Highway 4 and drive three miles; take the Alhambra Avenue exit and drive south to the Park and Ride lot on the right.

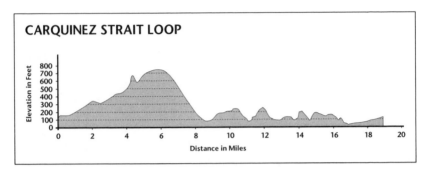

CARQUINEZ STRAIT LOOP

Route Directions for Carquinez Strait Loop

0.0 Park at the Park and Ride lot at the junction of Alhambra Avenue and Franklin Canyon Road. Ride west on Franklin Canyon Road. *Supplies are available in Walnut Creek, Concord, or Martinez.*

4.4 RIGHT on Cummings Skyway.

6.5 RIGHT on Crockett Boulevard.

8.5 RIGHT on Pomona Street into downtown Crockett; Pomona Street becomes Carquinez Scenic Drive just outside of town. *Supplies are available in downtown Crockett.*

10.3 Carquinez Regional Strait Shoreline on the left (Bull Valley Staging Area). *You can lock up your bike and hike the one-mile Carquinez Overlook Loop Trail.*

12.5 Road closure; ride around the gate.

14.2 Road is open to cars again.

16.4 RIGHT on Talbart Street.

16.5 LEFT on Escobar Street.

16.6 RIGHT on Berrellessa Street (becomes Alhambra Avenue).

18.5 Arrive at starting point.

26. BRIONES CREST LOOP

Briones Regional Park near Orinda
26A (Single Loop)

Type of trail:  dirt road and single-track

Difficulty: 🥾🥾🥾🥾🥾   **Total distance:** 8 miles

Riding time: 1.5 hours   **Elevation gain:** 1,200 feet

26B (Double Loop)

Type of trail: dirt road and single-track

Difficulty: 🥾🥾🥾🥾🥾   **Total distance:** 13.5 miles

Riding time: 2 hours   **Elevation gain:** 1,800 feet

Briones Regional Park is nearly 6,000 acres of grasslands and oaks that was once part of Rancho San Felipe, a Spanish land grant. In the mid-1800s, it was an important fruit-growing region. Today it's the grassy home of grazing cows and frequently visited by mountain bikers, dog walkers, hikers, and horseback riders.

The park is well known for its sunny exposure, numerous dirt roads, and

Briones Regional Park contains nearly 6,000 acres of rolling grassland hills.

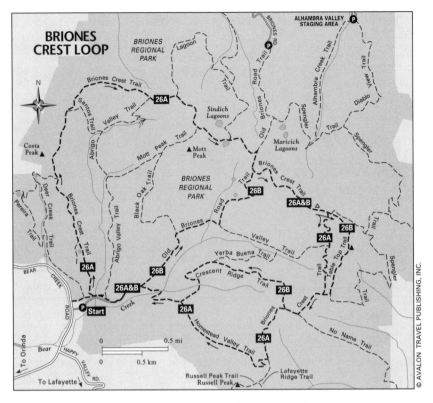

large expanse of open grasslands. Bordered on three sides by freeways—Highway 4, I-680, and Highway 2—it's an oasis of open space in a heavily urbanized area.

Because of an absence of shade in the park, summer is not the best time for riding here. It can be as hot as Hades on August afternoons, although quite pleasant in winter, spring, and fall. Note that cows roam the Briones pasturelands, so you must pass through a number of cattle gates. And those same cows are notorious for rutting the heck out of the ranch roads, so expect a lot of bumps, especially on the downhills.

Briones Crest Loop is the most popular ride at this park for mountain bikers. I've written it as a double loop that can be split up into two rides. The first half mile on wide single-track is a grunt of a climb (three short hills with a total 400-foot elevation gain), but beyond that, the remaining hills are more moderate. Most of the ride is on wide ranch roads, which lend themselves to some fun downhills. The final descent on Crescent Ridge Trail (Ride 26B only) is memorably steep.

Don't forget to pause for a moment at mile 4.3, where you pass Briones Peak, the highest point in the park at 1,483 feet. The hilltop affords great views of mighty Mount Diablo.

For more information, contact East Bay Regional Park District, 510/635-0135 or 510/562-7275, website: www.ebparks.org.

Driving Directions

From I-580 in Oakland, take Highway 24 east. Go through the Caldecott Tunnel and continue another 1.5 miles. Take the Orinda exit, then turn left on Camino Pablo and drive north for two miles. Turn right on Bear Creek Road and drive 4.4 miles, then turn right into Briones Regional Park/Bear Creek Staging Area entrance. Turn left just past the kiosk and park in the lower parking lot.

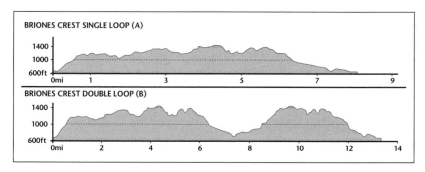

Route Directions for Briones Crest 26A (Single Loop)

0.0 Park at the lower parking lot at the Bear Creek Staging Area. The trailhead is at the end of the parking lot on the left. Follow Briones Crest Trail. *Water is available at the trailhead. Supplies are available in Orinda.*

0.1 RIGHT at Y-junction onto Briones Crest Trail.

0.5 End of the climb; trail widens and levels out.

1.1 STRAIGHT on Briones Crest Trail at junction with Deer Creek Trail. Stay straight on Briones Crest Trail at next four junctions.

3.3 Pass by Sindicich Lagoons (ranch ponds).

3.5 RIGHT on Old Briones Road.

3.6 LEFT on Briones Crest Trail.

4.3 Briones Peak, elevation 1,483 feet.

4.4 RIGHT to stay on Briones Crest Trail.

4.8 STRAIGHT on Briones Crest Trail.

5.7 STRAIGHT on Briones Crest Trail.

6.2 RIGHT on Homestead Valley Trail.

7.7 LEFT on Old Briones Road.

7.8 Go around gate and pass upper parking lot.

7.9 RIGHT at kiosk into lower parking lot.

8.0 Arrive at starting point.

Route Directions for 26B (Double Loop)

Follow the route directions for 26A to mile 7.7, then continue:

7.7 RIGHT on Old Briones Road.

8.6 LEFT to stay on Old Briones Road.

9.3 RIGHT on Briones Crest Trail (pass Briones Peak again).

10.1 STRAIGHT on Table Top Trail; head for radio antennas.

10.8 RIGHT to stay on Table Top Trail.

10.9 STRAIGHT on Briones Crest Trail.

11.3 RIGHT on Crescent Ridge Trail (head past the archery range).

12.7 RIGHT on Homestead Valley Trail.

13.2 LEFT on Old Briones Road.

13.3 Go around gate and pass upper parking lot.

13.4 RIGHT at kiosk into lower parking lot.

13.5 Arrive at starting point.

27. THREE BEARS LOOP

near San Pablo Reservoir and Orinda

Type of trail: paved roads with moderate car traffic

Difficulty: 𝗜 𝗜 𝗜 𝟙 𝟙

Total distance: 19.5 miles

Riding time: 1.5 hours

Elevation gain: 1,600 feet

Every serious East Bay cyclist has his or her own version of the Three Bears ride, with a variety of starting points and mileage totals. But what all those rides have in common is a heart-pumping, aerobic "crank" up the triumvirate of hills on Bear Valley Road, affectionately known as Papa Bear, Mama Bear, and Baby Bear.

This is one of the shorter versions of that classic ride, perfect for after work or any time you want a workout on the bike without taking up a whole day. By starting and ending near downtown Orinda, you can complete the Three Bears Loop in just under 20 miles. The loop can be ridden in either direction. As it is described here, you face Mama Bear first (450-foot climb), Papa Bear second (500-foot climb), and save the easiest hill for last (only 100-feet for the Baby). In between, there is a rest stop at Briones

A cyclist makes his way up "Papa Bear" on the Three Bears Loop near Orinda.

Regional Park, where you can fill up your water bottles or have a seat at a shady picnic table.

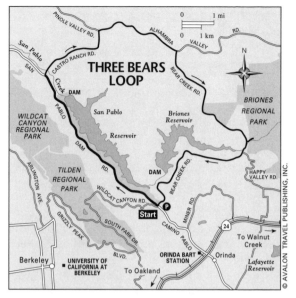

With the exception of the first leg on busy San Pablo Dam Road, and a short stretch through a cluster of red-tiled-roof subdivisions, most of the loop is on quiet back roads surrounded by open space. Bike lanes and wide shoulders make riding here stress-free. A highlight of this ride is its lovely views of two of the East Bay Municipal Utility District's reservoirs: San Pablo and Briones. In June, the roadside buckeye trees are in full bloom, wafting their sweet aroma through the air. The grasslands and chaparral plants emit their own pungent smell as they dry in the summer heat. You're far more likely to see quail and deer crossing the road than a parade of cars. This is the kind of pleasant ride you can do again and again, any time you're in the mood for a little exercise.

Driving Directions

From I-580 in Oakland, take Highway 24 east. Go through the Caldecott Tunnel and continue another 1.5 miles. Take the Orinda exit, then turn left on Camino Pablo and drive north for two miles. Turn right on Bear Creek Road and park in the pullout immediately on the left. (If this pullout is full, you can park in downtown Orinda, 1.6 miles south on Camino Pablo Road, then ride to this point.)

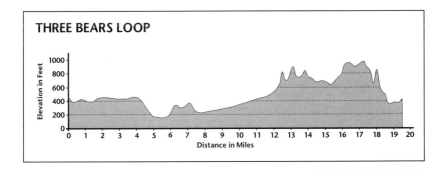

THREE BEARS LOOP

Route Directions for Three Bears Loop

0.0 Park at the top of Bear Creek Road, near its junction with Camino Pablo/San Pablo Dam Road. Ride out to Camino Pablo/San Pablo Dam Road. *Supplies are available 1.6 miles south in Orinda.*

0.1 RIGHT on San Pablo Dam Road.

5.4 RIGHT on Castro Ranch Road.

7.6 RIGHT on Alhambra Valley Road.

10.4 RIGHT on Bear Creek Road.

11.9 Start up Mama Bear.

13.0 Top of Mama Bear.

14.3 LEFT at Briones Regional Park Bear Creek Staging Area. *Water is available.* TURN AROUND.

14.9 LEFT on Bear Creek Road.

15.2 Start up Papa Bear.

17.4 Top of Papa Bear.

18.9 Start up Baby Bear.

19.5 Arrive at starting point (top of Baby Bear).

28. LAFAYETTE-MORAGA REGIONAL TRAIL

near Lafayette and Moraga

Type of trail:  paved bike path

Difficulty: 🍼🍼🍼🍼🍼

Total distance: 15.4 miles

Riding time: 1.5 hours

Elevation gain: 550 feet

When suburbs grow so large that they connect town to town without any buffer of open land between them, one of the smartest things city planners can do is create spaces where people can get a little fresh air and sunshine—places protected from cars, traffic, and urban noise. The Lafayette-Moraga Trail is such a place, and it is used by more than half a million people per year.

It's not exactly a trip to the wilderness, but you will see plenty of squirrels along the trail—not plain old Bay Area gray squirrels, but cute and chubby red squirrels with shiny, rust-colored coats. I spotted some busily burying nuts in flower beds, their genetic instinct preparing

The Lafayette-Moraga Regional Trail was opened in 1976 as one of America's first 500 converted rail trails.

them for the long, hard, snow-bound winter that will never come to sunny Moraga.

Also in the cute category, an entire pack of cub scouts cycled by me, dressed in their smart navy blue uniforms and tiny bicycle helmets. That's the kind of trail this is. A stretch of the old San Francisco-Sacramento Railroad, the path retains some of its railroad history with white crossing signs proudly displayed at junctions around Lafayette.

Unfortunately, Lafayette-Moraga Trail is intersected by several roads. Only one, St. Mary's Road, is likely to have much traffic. Beyond this crossing, you leave most of the neighborhoods behind and see less of St. Mary's Road (which parallels the trail up to this crossing). The trail passes St. Mary's College, which has a pretty white church tower set in the hillside and is surrounded by green playing fields. Shortly thereafter is Moraga Commons, a town park with a play area, restrooms, par course, and the like. A waterfall sculpture is located near a sign noting that Lafayette-Moraga Trail was opened in 1976 as one of America's first 500 rail trails. The trail's final stretch leads out to the country, ending at the Valle Vista Staging Area on Canyon Road, where you turn around and head back.

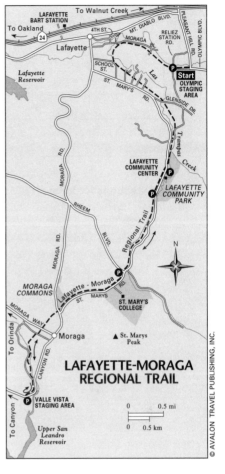

For more information, contact East Bay Regional Park District, 510/635-0135 or 510/562-7275, website: www.ebparks.org.

Driving Directions

From I-580 in Oakland, take Highway 24 east toward Walnut Creek. Go through the Caldecott Tunnel and take the Pleasant Hill Road exit south. Drive .7 miles to Olympic Boulevard and turn right. The parking lot is on the right in about 50 yards.

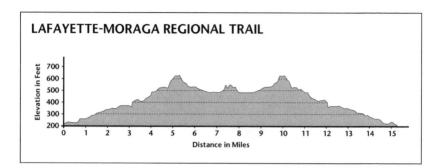

LAFAYETTE-MORAGA REGIONAL TRAIL

Elevation in Feet / *Distance in Miles*

Route Directions for Lafayette-Moraga Regional Trail

0.0 Park at Olympic staging area. *Water is available along the trail.*

1.1 STRAIGHT at junction with Briones-to-Las-Trampas Trail.

3.3 Cross St. Mary's Road.

3.4 Lafayette Community Center. *Water is available.*

5.2 St. Mary's College campus.

6.0 Moraga Commons park. *Water is available.*

7.7 Valle Vista staging area. TURN AROUND.

15.4 Arrive at starting point.

29. STEWARTVILLE & RIDGE TRAIL LOOP

Black Diamond Mines Regional Preserve near Antioch

Type of trail: dirt road

Difficulty: 𝐈 𝐈 𝐈 ⫰ ⫰

Total distance: 10.8 miles

Riding time: 2 hours

Elevation gain: 1,900 feet

From 1860 to 1906, the Mount Diablo Coal Field was the largest coal mining district in California. Located in what is now Black Diamond Mines Regional Preserve, this productive coal field on the northern side of Mount Diablo prompted the digging of 12 major mines and the growth of five townships. Much of this mining history, and a large acreage of rolling grassland hills and chaparral-clad slopes, is preserved at Black Diamond Mines (925/757-2620).

This loop ride reveals some of the park's highlights and adds some heart-pumping, leg-burning exercise to the bargain. Start with a mind-expanding trip to the park visitor center, then ride level Railroad Bed Trail to Stewartville Trail. A .5-mile ascent brings you to a cattle gate at a high point. Pass through the gate and admire the deep, grassy valley below you. The good news is that you're going to ride into that pretty valley; the bad news is that you'll have to climb back out of it.

Don't miss two spurs off the loop: Upper Old Canyon Trail, which leads steeply uphill to an overlook of the valley, and Tunnel Trail to Prospect Tunnel, an obvious gaping hole in the hillside. You can explore about 150 feet into the dark, cool mine shaft before you reach a steel gate. The shaft was driven in the 1860s by miners in search of coal or "black diamonds."

A mile past Tunnel Trail, make a sharp left turn on Ridge Trail, leaving the valley and beginning a steep, two-mile-long ascent. Ridge Trail roller-coasters along, dipping down occasionally but more often rising on very steep grades (the kind that may force you to walk your bike). The climb is eased by the sudden appearance of views to the north of Carquinez Strait, Suisun Bay, Pittsburg, and Antioch. Pause to enjoy the vistas while you catch your breath.

When at last Ridge Trail returns you to the gate at Stewartville Trail, consider a rest on the bench by the gate, where you can admire the rolling terrain you just explored. Then it's an easy 1.4 miles back to your car.

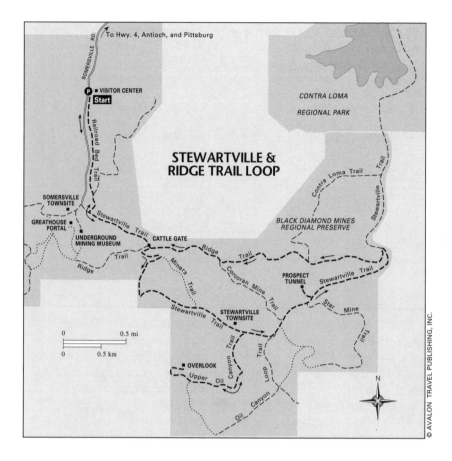

Because there is no technical single-track on this ride, it's tempting to bring beginning mountain bikers here. But unless they are very fit and ambitious, the many short but steep ascents will break their spirit. All riders should stay away from this park's trails when they are wet; the place is famous for its clay-like mud that can bring your wheels to a dead standstill, even on the downhills.

For more information, contact East Bay Regional Park District, 510/635-0135 or 510/562-7275, website: www.ebparks.org.

Driving Directions

From Highway 4 in Antioch, take the Somersville Road exit south. Drive three miles south on Somersville Road to the parking lot by the visitor center.

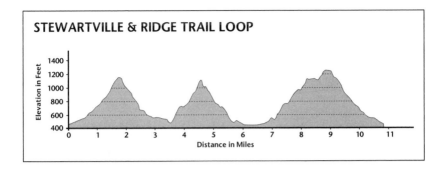

STEWARTVILLE & RIDGE TRAIL LOOP

Route Directions for Stewartville & Ridge Trail Loop

0.0 Park by the visitor center on Somersville Road. Take Railroad Bed Trail from the southern end of the parking lot. *Water is available at the visitor center; supplies are available four miles away in Antioch.*

0.7 LEFT on Stewartville Trail.

1.4 Cattle gate and viewpoint. Go through gate, then RIGHT to stay on Stewartville Trail; steep descent.

1.8 RIGHT at junction with Miners Trail to stay on Stewartville Trail.

3.2 RIGHT on Upper Oil Canyon Trail.

4.4 Arrive at overlook. TURN AROUND.

5.6 RIGHT to continue on Stewartville Trail.

6.1 LEFT on Tunnel Trail. Park your bike and walk into the dark tunnel, then TURN AROUND.

6.4 LEFT to continue on Stewartville Trail.

7.3 LEFT (very sharp turn) on Ridge Trail; steep climb begins.

9.4 RIGHT on Stewartville Trail at cattle gate.

10.1 RIGHT on Railroad Bed Trail.

10.8 Arrive at starting point.

30. EAST & WEST RIDGE LOOP

Redwood Regional Park near Oakland

Type of trail:  dirt road

Difficulty: ❚❚ ⌂⌂⌂

Total distance: 9.4 miles

Riding time: 2 hours

Elevation gain: 1,100 feet

They don't call this place Redwood Regional Park for nothing. The dark, shaggy-barked trees grow more than 100 feet tall and their shady canopy covers a vast expanse of the park. The redwoods are the second-generation offspring of the original trees that once towered over this canyon. Between 1840 and 1860, loggers felled these ancient giants to provide lumber for the growing cities of San Francisco and San Jose.

The redwoods aren't the only prizes of Redwood Regional Park. The park is bordered by two high ridges to the east and west, both of which offer expansive views. This loop ride, a standard for East Bay mountain bikers, travels out the East Ridge and back on West Ridge. Although the ride is entirely on wide dirt roads, it still presents some technical chal-

West Ridge Trail at Redwood Regional Park offers views of Oakland and San Francisco Bay to the west and Mount Diablo to the east.

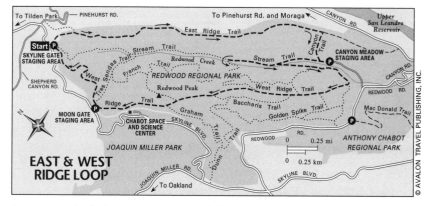

lenges, particularly on a steep, rutted downhill on Canyon Trail and a steep uphill on West Ridge Trail. Strong beginners should be able to handle it, or at least walk their bikes if they can't.

From the Skyline Gate staging area, follow East Ridge Trail generally downhill for three miles in a two-steps-down, one-step-up fashion, rolling along small hills. Watch for long-distance views of the reservoirs to the east. Turn right on Canyon Trail, drop steeply, then follow Stream Trail into the canyon to see up close some of the park's redwood stands. After a brief, level out-and-back on Stream Trail, you'll face a hearty climb on West Ridge Trail. The first .75 mile is the worst (400-foot gain), but the trail continues to ascend moderately for almost three miles.

West Ridge Trail's final stretch passes by the newly built observatory at the Chabot Space and Science Center (worth a visit). You'll catch fine glimpses of Oakland and San Francisco Bay to the west; equally good is the view to the east of looming Mount Diablo at 3,849 feet. The last mile is a delightfully easy cruise back to Skyline Gate through a shady forest of bay laurel, madrone, and Monterey pine.

For more information, contact East Bay Regional Park District, 510/635-0135 or 510/562-7275, website: www.ebparks.org.

Driving Directions

From I-580 in Oakland, take the 35th Avenue exit and turn north. Drive 2.4 miles (35th Avenue will become Redwood Road). Turn left on Skyline Boulevard and drive 3.7 miles to the Skyline Gate Staging Area, located at the intersection of Skyline and Pine Hills Drive. (Skyline Boulevard makes a sharp right turn after the first half mile.)

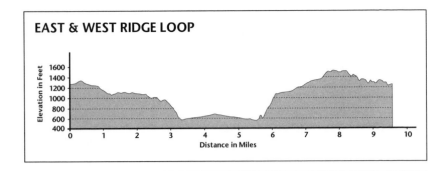

EAST & WEST RIDGE LOOP

Elevation in Feet — Distance in Miles

Route Directions for East & West Ridge Loop

0.0 Park at Skyline Gate staging area and take East Ridge Trail, the northernmost of three possible trails. *Water is available at the trailhead.*

2.9 RIGHT on Canyon Trail.

3.3 RIGHT on Stream Trail at Canyon Meadow Staging Area.

3.6 STRAIGHT at junction with Bridle Trail; you'll return to this intersection shortly.

4.2 End of bikes-allowed section of Stream Trail. TURN AROUND. *Stop at one of five picnic areas under the redwoods. Water is available.*

4.8 RIGHT on Bridle Trail upon return to previous junction.

5.0 RIGHT on West Ridge Trail; begin ascent to ridge.

6.3 RIGHT to stay on West Ridge Trail.

7.7 Chabot Space and Science Center.

9.4 Arrive at starting point.

31. WALL POINT & BARBEQUE TERRACE LOOP

Mount Diablo State Park near Danville

Type of trail: dirt roads

Difficulty: 𝟙𝟙𝟙

Total distance: 9.0 miles

Riding time: 2 hours

Elevation gain: 1,600 feet

Ride the Devil. That's the attitude of most mountain bikers who come to pedal on "devilish" Mount Diablo. The great 3,849-foot peak is a butt-kicker for casual riders, due to steep and rugged fire roads, occasional stretches of single-track that require advanced technical skills, and the brutally hot temperatures that occur on these slopes during four to five months of the year. That said, the Wall Point and Rock City Loop is one of the more manageable rides on the mountain, although it certainly has its share of ups and downs.

The trip starts at the Macedo Ranch Trailhead and begins with a moderate climb up Wall Point Road. This is followed by a rocky descent into Pine Canyon, which may present some technical challenges to the less skilled. This downhill is known as "the staircase" because of its layers of exposed rock. Pine Canyon is especially lovely in winter when its stream

© ANN MARIE BROWN

A tough climb on Barbeque Terrace Road leads to a rewarding view looking out over Pine Canyon.

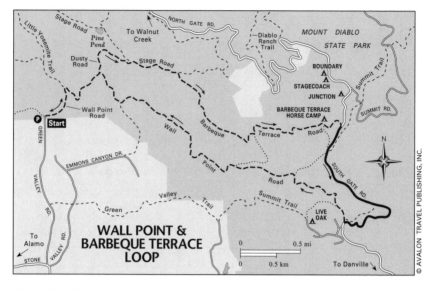

flows, but the wet season also necessitates a few creek crossings. After a series of winter storms, Pine Canyon sometimes becomes impassable. Call to check on trail conditions if you are visiting in the wet season.

A tough climb out of Pine Canyon ensues on Barbeque Terrace Road, in which you must gain 900 feet in little more than a mile, often on a loose, pebbly surface. After that memorable ascent, which leaves many riders walking their bikes and weeping in the Diablo dust, the trail ends at Barbeque Terrace Group Campground. Admire the view from the trail gate and congratulate yourself for having made it up this hellacious hill. Then ride up the paved camp access road to South Gate Road for a fast downhill on pavement to Rock City. (A short single-track option is also possible here.)

Lock up your bike and take a brief walk at Rock City. Set among clusters of tall manzanita, foothill pines, madrones, and live oaks, Rock City is a jumble of eroded sandstone outcroppings that was formed 40 or 50 million years ago during the Eocene period, when Mount Diablo was buried under a great sea. Eventually the waters receded and the remaining sand hardened into a ridge of rocks. This rocky ridge has been weathered and eroded by centuries of wind and rain, creating odd-shaped boulders with small caves and Swiss cheese–style holes. They're fun to look at and climb around on.

After exploring the rocks, loop back to Macedo Ranch on Wall Point Road, a wide fire road that runs along a rocky ridgeline. As you pedal west, you'll have lovely views of Rock City and "real" cities—Danville and Walnut Creek—to the west. You'll face a moderate climb for the first 1.6 miles, then it's downhill all the way back to the parking lot.

For more information, contact Mount Diablo State Park, 925/837-2525 or 925/837-0904, website: www.mdia.org.

Driving Directions

From I-680 at Danville, take the Diablo Road exit and head east. Follow Diablo Road for 1.4 miles (turn right at .7 mile to stay on Diablo Road), then turn left at Green Valley Road. Drive two miles to the end of Green Valley Road and the Macedo Ranch Trailhead.

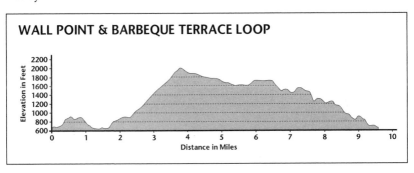

WALL POINT & BARBEQUE TERRACE LOOP

Route Directions for Wall Point & Barbeque Terrace Loop

0.0 Park at Macedo Ranch and start riding on the fire road by the signboard and water trough. This is Wall Point Road, but it is signed as "Macedo Ranch to Summit Trail." *Supplies are available in Danville.*

0.3 RIGHT to stay on Wall Point Road.

0.9 LEFT on Dusty Road/Pine Canyon Trail (Wall Point Road goes right).

1.4 RIGHT on Stage Road.

1.8 RIGHT on Barbeque Terrace Road.

2.6 Tough climb begins.

3.7 Barbecue Terrace Group Camp; follow paved camp road uphill to paved South Gate Road. *Water is available at the group camp.*

4.0 RIGHT on South Gate Road. *If you prefer to ride on dirt, you can pick up single-track Summit Trail .2 mile down South Gate Road on the right, signed as "multi-purpose trail."*

5.7 RIGHT at Rock City/Live Oak parking lot. *Lock up your bike and explore the fascinating rocks.* TURN AROUND. Ride 50 yards uphill (backtracking) on South Gate Road to the start of Wall Point Road (across from the private residence and service area).

5.8 LEFT on Wall Point Road. *Water is available at the service area across from the start of Wall Point Road.*

8.3 RIGHT to stay on Wall Point Road.

8.5 LEFT to stay on Wall Point Road.

9.4 Arrive at starting point.

32. MITCHELL & DONNER CANYONS LOOP

Mount Diablo State Park near Clayton
32A (Short Loop)

Type of trail: dirt roads

Difficulty: 𝐈𝐈𝐈◊◊

Total distance: 8.6 miles

Riding time: 1.5 hours

Elevation gain: 1600 feet

32B (Long Loop)

Type of trail: dirt roads and single-track

Difficulty: 𝐈𝐈𝐈𝐈◊

Total distance: 13.1 miles

Riding time: 2.5 hours

Elevation gain: 2900 feet

This ride on the "back" side of Mount Diablo isn't particularly long but it is quite strenuous. Still, the rewards are great: The loop passes by some of the most diverse habitats that the old Devil's Mountain has to offer, including gangly Coulter and foothill pines with their heavyweight cones, a wide range of chaparral plants (sage, toyon, manzanita, yerba santa, and more) and lush streamside vegetation. Plus, with the completion of every gut-thumping ascent on this route, you are rewarded with wide views of the surrounding area.

Mitchell Canyon Fire Road starts out deceptively easy, with a gentle climb along Mitchell Creek. But just past the two-mile mark, things start to get ugly, I mean challenging. Over the next three miles to Deer Flat, you'll gain 1,200 feet, much of it with average grades that reach into the mid-teens and almost no shade from the ruthless sun.

If you've had enough when you reach oak-shaded Deer Flat, you can always bail out and head back on Meridian Ridge Road, making an 8.6-mile loop (Ride 32A) with only a half-mile additional ascent. By choosing this option, you can add on a thrilling short hike to your day. Lock up your bike near Murchio Gap on Meridian Ridge Road and walk out and back on the Eagle Peak Trail to Eagle Peak, elevation 2,369 feet. The

Make sure you choose a cool day for riding the shadeless stretches of the Mitchell & Donner Canyons Loop.

.8-mile-long trail leads along the narrow backbone of Bald Ridge, with steep drop-offs on both sides. From Eagle Peak's rocky summit, you'll gain wide vistas of Mount Diablo's North Peak, the Sacramento and San Joaquin Delta, Honker Bay, and Suisun Bay. Although you have opted for the shorter bike ride, after visiting this impressive summit you can call yourself a real mountaineer.

Meanwhile, the intrepid cyclist on Ride 32B continues on a 1,000-foot climb to Juniper Campground and the paved Summit Road, then climbs some more, this time on blessed, smooth pavement, to a 3,400-foot-high point called the Devils Elbow. Here, single-track lovers will be thrilled by North Peak Trail's one mile of technically tricky stuff, which throws plenty of rocks and tree roots in your path as it makes a speedy descent to a saddle at Prospectors Gap. This is a good place to repeat to yourself the Smart Mountain Biker's Mantra: "Caution is the better part of valor." This is also a good place to slow down and enjoy the views, which extend southwest to the windmills in Livermore and east to the Central Valley. You pass directly below the large rock outcrop called Devils Pulpit on Mount Diablo's summit.

At Prospectors Gap, 32B riders follow yet another fire road very steeply downhill to join their friends who went for the shorter Ride 32A. Together everyone cruises down Meridian Ridge Road to Meridian Point, an overlook with a wide view of Clayton and a glimpse at Suisun Bay to the northwest. Then it's onward to Donner Canyon Road, Murchio Road, and back to the trailhead at Mitchell Canyon.

For more information, contact Mount Diablo State Park, 925/837-2525 or 925/837-0904, website: www.mdia.org.

Driving Directions

From I-680 heading north in Walnut Creek, take the Ygnacio Valley Road exit. Drive east on Ygnacio Valley Road for 7.5 miles to Clayton Road. Turn right (south) on Clayton

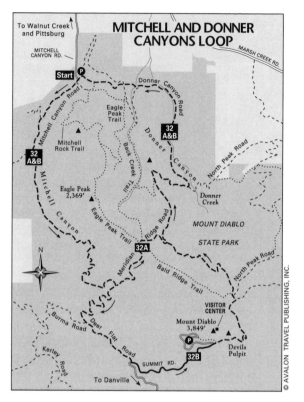

Road and drive 1.5 miles to Mitchell Canyon Road. Turn right and drive to the end of the road and the trailhead.

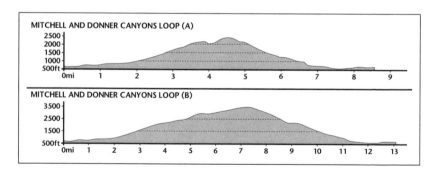

Route Directions for Ride 32A (Mitchell and Donner Canyons Short Loop)

0.0 Park at the Mitchell Canyon Trailhead and begin riding on Mitchell Canyon Road. *Supplies are available in Clayton.*

2.0 Begin serious climb.

3.8 LEFT on Meridan Ridge Road at Deer Flat (three-way junction); keep climbing.

4.5 Eagle Peak Trail on left. *Lock up your bike and walk the .8-mile Eagle Peak Trail to the 2,369-foot summit.*

4.9 LEFT to stay on Meridian Ridge Road at junction with Prospectors Gap Road.

6.3 LEFT on Donner Canyon Road at junction with Cardinet Oaks Road.

7.6 LEFT on Murchio Road; stay straight at next three junctions.

8.6 Arrive at starting point.

Route Directions for 32B (Mitchell and Donner Canyons Long Loop)

Follow the route directions for 32A to mile 3.8, then continue:

3.8 RIGHT on Deer Flat Road at Deer Flat (three-way junction).

4.9 LEFT to stay on Deer Flat Road at junction with Burma Road.

5.4 Juniper Campground; follow the paved camp road out to Summit Road. *Water is available at Juniper Campground.*

5.6 LEFT on paved Summit Road.

7.1 RIGHT on North Peak Trail (single-track) at hairpin turn in road (Devils Elbow).

8.1 LEFT on Prospectors Gap Road.

9.4 RIGHT on Meridian Ridge Road.

10.8 LEFT on Donner Canyon Road at junction with Cardinet Oaks Road.

12.1 LEFT on Murchio Road; stay straight at next three junctions.

13.1 Arrive at starting point.

33. MOUNT DIABLO SUMMIT RIDE

Blackhawk to Mount Diablo Summit

Type of trail:  paved roads with moderate car traffic

Difficulty: 🍶🍶🍶🍶🍶

Total distance: 29.6 miles

Riding time: 4–5 hours

Elevation gain: 3,200 feet

Almost everybody thinks about making the trip to 3,849-foot Mount Diablo from time to time. After all, you see it from just about everywhere in the Bay Area. It's not the tallest mountain around San Francisco Bay (Mount Hamilton near San Jose is 360 feet taller; see Ride 57), but it has a way of making its presence known, looming in the background of the lives of millions of East Bay residents.

Although most people travel to the summit of Mount Diablo by car, a better way to get there is by bike. Sure, it's a long grind with a nearly non-stop elevation gain, but this is what you live for, right? You haven't really experienced Diablo's Summit Road until you've ridden it on a bike. With every curve in the winding pavement, the views are constantly changing.

With every curve in the winding pavement that leads to the summit of Mount Diablo, the vistas are constantly changing.

Two roads—North Gate and South Gate—travel most of the way up the mountain; they join at Summit Ranger station for the final 4.5 miles on Summit Road to the top. This ride follows South Gate Road from Blackhawk, elevation 738 feet; it's the easier of the two roads. Slightly easier, anyway. If you want to shorten this ride, just drive your car farther up the mountain road and start from one of the parking areas within the state park, like Curry Point or Rock City.

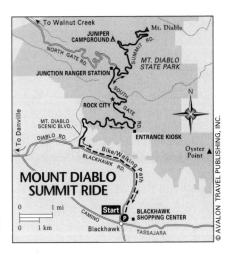

Pick a cool day (forget summer on this shadeless "devil's mountain") and be encouraged by the fact that water and rest stops are plentiful all the way up the mountain (most roadside picnic areas and campgrounds have water).

For more information, contact Mount Diablo State Park, 925/837-2525 or 925/837-0904, website: www.mdia.org.

Driving Directions

From the junction of I-680 and I-580 in Dublin, drive north on I-680 for five miles to the Crow Canyon Road exit. Drive east for four miles; Crow Canyon Road becomes Blackhawk Road at its junction with Tassajara Road. Park at or near Blackhawk Plaza shopping center and ride east on Blackhawk Road.

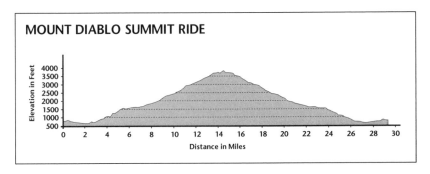

Route Directions for Mount Diablo Summit Ride

0.0 Park at or near Blackhawk Plaza shopping center and ride east on Blackhawk Road, then pick up the bike/walking path alongside the road. *Supplies are available at this shopping center.*

3.4 RIGHT on Mount Diablo Scenic Boulevard.

4.5 Mount Diablo State Park gate.

7.1 Entrance kiosk.

7.6 Rock City region of the park.

8.2 Rock City parking area (good alternate starting point).

8.8 Curry Point parking area.

10.3 RIGHT on Summit Road at Junction Ranger Station.

12.8 Juniper Campground.

14.8 Mount Diablo summit. TURN AROUND.

29.6 Arrive at starting point.

34. ROUND VALLEY RAMBLE

Round Valley Regional Preserve near Clayton

Type of trail:  dirt road

Difficulty: 🔲 Ï Ö Ö Ö **Total distance:** 10.8 miles (or longer options)

Riding time: 1.5 hours **Elevation gain:** 600 feet

If you ever start to feel like the East Bay is too crowded, too congested, and has too much concrete, take a trip a little farther east to the back side of Mount Diablo. Here on the far eastern edge of the San Francisco Bay Area are wide open spaces, spring wildflowers, and stately oak trees.

You'll find all this and more at Round Valley Regional Preserve, the 2,000-acre home of nesting golden eagles, burrowing owls, chubby ground squirrels, and the endangered San Joaquin kit fox. The bike riding here is mellow and easy, unless of course you show up at midday in August, when it can be more than 100 degrees.

From the preserve staging area, the trail starts out with a long bridge over Marsh Creek. At the far side of the bridge, a right turn puts you on Miwok Trail. Immediately you face the only real hill of the day; the remaining miles of this ride are mostly level.

In .5 mile, the wide dirt road meets up with Round Valley Creek. If

The old ranch roads at Round Valley provide gentle trails for riders of all abilities.

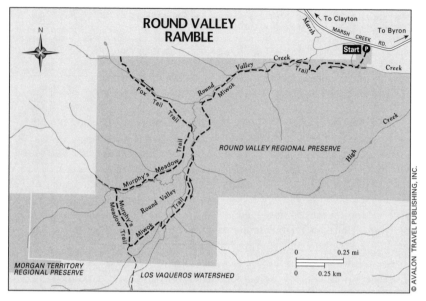

you've timed your trip for the wet season, the stream will run cool and clear alongside you for much of your ride. You'll notice the remains of old farming equipment along the dirt trail; this land was farmed by the Murphy family from 1873 until 1988, when it was donated to the East Bay Regional Park District.

Stay on Miwok Trail through the entire length of the preserve, then turn right on Murphy's Meadow Trail. You'll loop back on the far side of Round Valley Creek. At a junction with Fox Tail Trail, follow Fox Tail Trail uphill for a short out-and-back excursion. Head for the top of the hill, where you'll find a wide view of rolling hills and vast, unpopulated parkland. What a fine spot for a picnic lunch.

Riders looking for more mileage can follow Miwok Trail out of the park, through a 1.6-mile stretch of Los Vaqueros Watershed, and into the east side of Morgan Territory Regional Preserve, where most trails are open to mountain bikes (see the following trail description). Free maps available from the East Bay Regional Park District (510/562-7275 or 510/635-0135, website: www.ebparks.org) can get you where you want to go.

Driving Directions

From I-580 in Livermore, take the Vasco Road exit and drive north 13 miles. Turn left (west) on Camino Diablo Road and drive 3.5 miles. Where Camino Diablo ends, continue straight on Marsh Creek Road for 1.5 miles to the Round Valley parking area on the left.

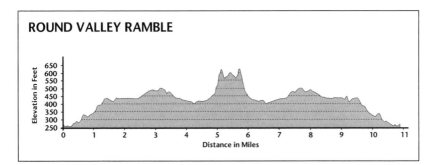

ROUND VALLEY RAMBLE

Route Directions for Round Valley Ramble

0.0 Park at Round Valley staging area and ride across the bridge. *Supplies are available in Clayton, eight miles west.*

0.1 RIGHT on Miwok Trail at far side of bridge.

0.5 STRAIGHT at junction with trail on right.

2.8 RIGHT on Murphy's Meadow Trail. *Miwok Trail leaves the park here, travels through the Los Vaqueros Watershed and into Morgan Territory Regional Preserve, for more riding options.*

3.7 RIGHT to stay on Murphy's Meadow Trail.

4.6 LEFT on Fox Tail Trail.

5.4 End of Fox Tail Trail. TURN AROUND.

10.8 Arrive at starting point.

35. VOLVON & VALLEY VIEW LOOP

Morgan Territory Regional Preserve near Livermore

Type of trail:  dirt road

Difficulty: 🥾🥾🥾   **Total distance:** 8.4 miles

Riding time: 2 hours   **Elevation gain:** 1,200 feet

Morgan Territory—even the name sounds wild, like a holdover from the Old West. If you're wondering if anything wild could still exist in Contra Costa County, wonder no more. Come to Morgan Territory and rediscover the wild East Bay.

The drive to the trailhead is a trip in itself. Follow narrow, winding Morgan Territory Road north of Livermore to the preserve's main trailhead. Try not to get so wowed by the views that you drive right off the curvy, narrow road.

At the trailhead parking lot, you've climbed to 1,900 feet in elevation. (Okay, so your car has done the work.) Hopefully you've planned your visit for the cooler months of the year, because the open hills

Morgan Territory's rolling hills are punctuated by magnificent oak trees and colorful spring wildflowers.

around Livermore bake in the summer. If you're riding in the warm season, make sure it is *very* early in the morning. Pick up a free trail map at the trailhead (the preserve has an overabundance of trail junctions) and follow Volvon Trail uphill and through a cattle gate.

A succession of trails—Volvon, Blue Oak, and Valley View—carry you up and down Morgan Territory's scenic, rolling hills, which are punctuated by magnificent oak

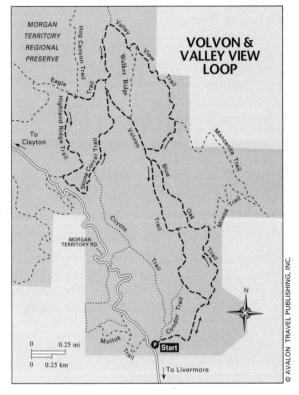

trees and colorful lichen-coated rocks. In the spring, more than 90 wildflower species blossom along these grassy hillsides. Views to the west of Mount Diablo are fine, but what is most surprising is Valley View Trail's eastern perspective on the San Joaquin Valley. On the clearest days of winter, the snow-capped High Sierra can be seen, more than 100 miles away.

The route described below makes a dogleg from Valley View to cruise a section of 1,700-foot Highland Ridge, where more views are yours for the taking. The final stretch of the route is a long, mostly level cruise back to the trailhead on Volvon Trail. Overall, the riding is generally easy here, with wide trails and few technical challenges except for the ruts and holes caused by the trampling feet of cattle. You'll probably see a few groups of cud-chewing bovines somewhere along the path. They usually flee from mountain bikers, or stop in mid-chew to stare at you.

For more information, contact East Bay Regional Park District, 510/635-0135 or 510/562-7275, website: www.ebparks.org.

Driving Directions

From I-580 in Livermore, take the North Livermore Avenue exit and turn north. Drive north for four miles, then turn right on Morgan Territory Road. Drive 5.6 miles to the entrance to Morgan Territory Preserve on the right. (The road is narrow and steep.)

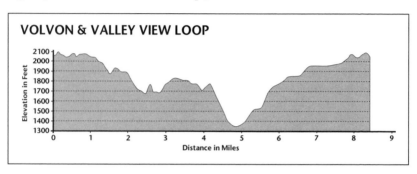

VOLVON & VALLEY VIEW LOOP

Route Directions for Volvon & Valley View Loop

0.0 Park at Morgan Territory Preserve trailhead. Start riding on the main, wide trail (Volvon Trail). *Supplies are available in Livermore; stock up before you drive out Morgan Territory Road.*

0.3 LEFT, then immediately RIGHT on Blue Oak Trail.

1.7 STRAIGHT on Volvon Trail.

1.8 RIGHT on Valley View Trail.

3.0 RIGHT on Volvon Loop Trail.

3.7 RIGHT on Eagle Trail.

4.1 LEFT on Highland Ridge Trail.

5.0 LEFT on Stone Corral Trail just before Highland Ridge Trail meets paved road.

6.1 RIGHT on Volvon Trail; stay on Volvon Trail at next several junctions.

8.0 RIGHT, then immediately RIGHT again to stay on Volvon Trail.

8.4 Arrive at starting point.

36. LAKE CHABOT LOOP

Lake Chabot and Anthony Chabot Regional Parks
east of San Leandro

Type of trail: 🐴 🚲 dirt road and paved bike path

Difficulty: ▮▮◌◌◌   **Total distance:** 13.3 miles (or 9-mile option)

Riding time: 2 hours   **Elevation gain:** 1,100 feet

Lakeside trails are often level and somewhat predictable, but the trails around Lake Chabot never stop turning, twisting, climbing, and diving. You're either braking hard or pedaling hard the whole way. Still, with only 800 feet of elevation gain, the Lake Chabot Loop is suitable for all kinds of riders. The challenge of a few hills is compensated by the sheer fun of the ride. This is a good place to gain some experience on a mountain bike.

You will have to put up with some irritating signs of civilization, though. In addition to the lake's busy marina and campground, you'll ride near a golf course and a shooting range. And if this is your first time here, you must pay careful attention to trail junctions. There are a ton of them.

© ANN MARIE BROWN

The popular bike trail around Lake Chabot is a mix of pavement, fire roads, and single-track.

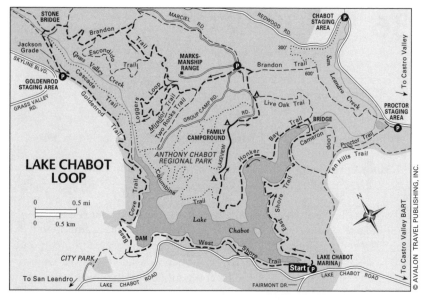

An advantage to the prolific junctions is that Lake Chabot's trails can be customized according to your desires and abilities. The route described here combines the paved West and East Shore trails with several dirt fire roads for a 13.3-mile round-trip. Families with young children and skinny-tire riders will want to stick to pavement for a nine-mile out-and-back. The paved trails skirt the lake's edge, sometimes rising up along its steep walls, sometimes tracing a line just a few feet from the water.

Following the loop below, East Shore Trail's pavement ends 1.8 miles beyond the marina. Mountain bikers continue onward, walking their bikes over a bridge to connect with Honker Bay Trail (some use Live Oak Trail to make their loop; I prefer Honker Bay because it stays along the lakeshore). Take a trail map with you to negotiate the long stretch of Brandon Trail; it intersects annoyingly with what seems like a million other trails. Still, it offers some wide views of San Francisco Bay.

If you want to turn your bike ride into a day at the lake, Lake Chabot Marina (510/582-2198) has boats for rent, plus a small café that sells hot dogs and coffee. Lake Chabot is stocked with trout, bass, and catfish, and fishing prospects are quite good.

For more information, contact East Bay Regional Park District, 510/635-0135 or 510/562-7275, website: www.ebparks.org.

Driving Directions

From Oakland, drive east on I-580 and take the Dutton/Estudillo Avenue exit in San Leandro. Drive .5 mile, then turn left on Estudillo Avenue and drive .4 mile. Bear right at the "Y" with Lake Chabot Road and drive 2.5 miles to a T-junction. Turn left, then left again into the marina.

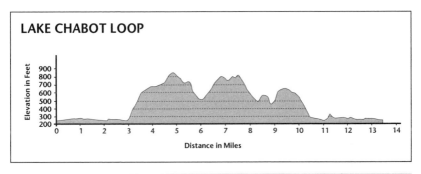

Route Directions for Lake Chabot Loop

0.0 Park at Lake Chabot Marina and head for the east side of the picnic area to the start of East Shore Trail. *Supplies are available at the marina store and café.* A trail map is posted on a signboard next to the marina café.

1.8 LEFT across narrow bridge at end of paved East Shore Trail; walk your bike.

1.9 LEFT on Honker Bay Trail.

3.5 Join paved campground road; ride through family campground on main road.

4.0 RIGHT on Towhee Trail.

4.8 LEFT on Brandon Trail (easy to miss—watch for it!).

4.9 Parking lot and restrooms; cross road and pick up Brandon Trail on other side.

5.5 LEFT on Logger's Loop Trail (or RIGHT to stay on Brandon Trail and save .9 mile).

6.6 Back on Brandon Trail.

8.4 LEFT and across stone bridge to LEFT on Jackson Grade to Goldenrod Trail.

8.8 Grass Valley Staging Area; stay on Goldenrod Trail.

10.2 RIGHT on Bass Cove Trail.

11.5 LEFT on paved West Shore Trail.

13.3 Arrive at starting point.

37. PALOMARES ROAD

east of Hayward and Fremont

Type of trail:  paved road with minimal car traffic

Difficulty: 𝗜𝗜𝗜

Total distance: 20.2 miles

Riding time: 1–2 hours   **Elevation gain:** 1,900 feet

For a short stint of my life, I had the pleasure of living in the peaceful Sunol countryside, where on Sunday mornings I would awaken to the sounds of birds chirping and my roommate yelling, "Get up! Let's go ride Palomares Road."

And so we did, along with dozens of other East Bay cyclists, almost every Sunday, rain or shine. It was a happy habit that put some "country" into our urban lives.

The good news is that Palomares Road is still a peaceful country road, despite the fact that it's bordered by busy highways on both ends. It's perfect for a quick 20-mile training ride after work or on the weekends, and

Palomares Road is a peaceful country lane bordered by busy highways on both ends.

feels like a getaway even though it's very close to home for riders in the southeast Bay Area.

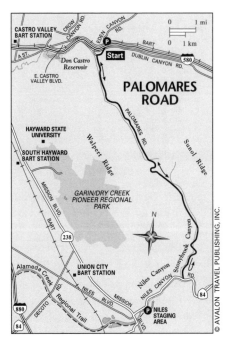

Some cyclists make a loop out of Palomares Road by riding Dublin Canyon Road to the north and Niles Canyon Road (Highway 84) to the south, then using Foothill Road as the east connector. I don't recommend it. These three roads were viable for cyclists a decade or so ago, but are now heavily trafficked almost 24 hours a day. Besides, who wants to ride on a freeway frontage road after spinning though Palomares Road's lovely forested scenery?

Palomares Road ascends from both ends; the high point is almost exactly in the middle. That means you get an invigorating climb and a fun descent in both directions. In between, you have many rolling curves and a chance to ride as fast as 40 mph on the downhills, if you so choose.

If you're more into savoring your rides than speeding through them, note that two wineries are now open on Palomares Road: Chouinard Winery (open weekends only, 510/582-9900) and Westover Vineyards (open daily, 510/885-1501).

Driving Directions

From Hayward, drive four miles east on I-580 and take the Eden Canyon Road/Palomares Road exit. Turn left, cross under the freeway, and park on the north side of the freeway in the dirt pullout (start of Eden Canyon Road).

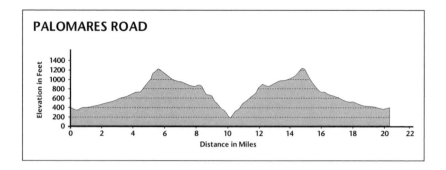

Route Directions for Palomares Road

0.0 Park in the dirt pullout at the start of Eden Canyon Road, by the I-580 freeway overpass. Ride under the overpass and cross Dublin Canyon Road to access Palo Verde Road. *Supplies are available in Hayward or Dublin.*

0.4 LEFT on Palomares Road.

5.4 Summit of Palomares Road.

6.3 Chouinard Winery.

6.6 Westover Vineyards.

10.1 End of Palomares Road at Highway 84. TURN AROUND.

20.2 Arrive at starting point.

38. MORGAN TERRITORY ROAD

Livermore to Clayton

Type of trail:  paved roads with minimal car traffic

Difficulty: 𝐼𝐼𝐼𝐼𝐼

Total distance: 46.2 miles

Riding time: 3–4 hours

Elevation gain: 3,500 feet

One of the finest roads in the East Bay crosses through the Black Hills north of Livermore and passes by the eastern flank of mighty Mount Diablo and neighboring North Peak. Morgan Territory Road, as it is known, leaves the shopping centers and I-580 freeway traffic far behind as it carves a narrow path through hillside grasslands and scenic oak woodlands. If the hustle and bustle of the East Bay has started to wear you down, you need a ride on Morgan Territory Road.

As an out-and-back ride, this route from Livermore to Clayton has a good hill climb in both directions, so a stop in Clayton for lunch is recommended, and also perhaps a rest stop near the road's summit at elevation 2,100 feet, near Morgan Territory Regional Preserve. Your main concern is the weather—this kind of climbing in these sunny, exposed

Morgan Territory Road is only one lane wide.

hills should be reserved for the cooler days of fall, winter, and spring. Another concern is the narrowness of Morgan Territory Road; one car and one bike makes a crowd. Fortunately, cars are few and far between.

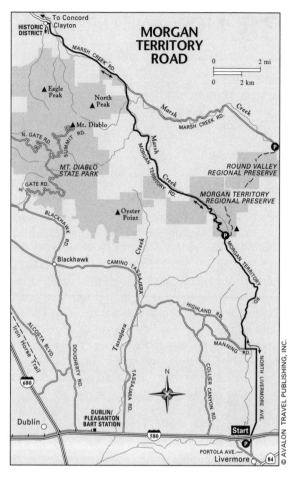

Although it seems sensible to make a loop out of this ride by returning from Clayton to Livermore on Marsh Creek Road and Vasco Road, a five-mile stretch of Vasco Road has been widened in recent years, making it as fast and hectic as a freeway. Intrepid riders may still want to make this loop, but be forewarned of the long hill climb on Vasco Road with cars peeling by you at 70 mph. Although the road's shoulder is wide, riding it is just plain stressful. An out-and-back on Morgan Territory Road is safer, more scenic, and far more relaxing.

For more information on the parks in this area, contact East Bay Regional Park District, 510/635-0135 or 510/562-7275, website: www.ebparks.org.

Driving Directions

From Livermore on I-580, take the North Livermore Avenue exit and park at the shopping center just south of I-580 on North Livermore Avenue.

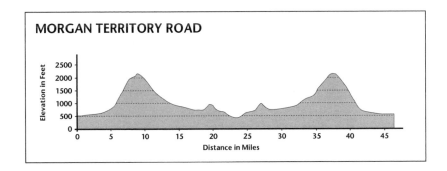

MORGAN TERRITORY ROAD

Route Directions for Morgan Territory Road

0.0 Park at the shopping center just south of I-580 on North Livermore Avenue and ride north, crossing under the freeway. Set your odometer on the north side of I-580. *Supplies are available in Livermore.*

3.5 LEFT on Manning Road.

4.0 RIGHT on Morgan Territory Road.

4.7 Road narrows to single lane.

9.5 Entrance to Morgan Territory Regional Preserve on right.

15.0 Road widens to two lanes.

18.7 LEFT on Marsh Creek Road.

22.7 LEFT on Marsh Creek Road (also called Clayton Road in Clayton).

23.2 Arrive in Clayton historic district. TURN AROUND. *Supplies are available in Clayton.*

46.2 Arrive at starting point.

39. LIVERMORE WINERY RIDE

Livermore

Type of trail:  paved roads with moderate car traffic

Difficulty: 🍶🍶🍶🍶🍶

Total distance: 19.5 miles

Riding time: 2 hours

Elevation gain: 800 feet

The town of Livermore, well known for being the home of Lawrence Livermore Laboratories and a huge collection of windmills, was founded in 1869 as a farming community. Cattle and sheep ranching and hay and grain production made the fertile area prosperous for more than a century. Even today the annual June rodeo is still the biggest show in town, although Livermore's agricultural legacy has largely shifted to vineyards and wine production. All the better for cyclists, who can ride this easy tour of rolling hills and stop to taste the products of nearly a dozen wineries.

While planning your ride, remember two things: First, if you want to do much wine tasting, ride on Saturday or Sunday, because many smaller wineries are not open on weekdays. Second, consider the weather in Livermore. Pick a cool day and bring along a picnic for the ride's finale, when you return to shady Sycamore Grove Park (925/373-5770).

If you feel like riding a bit more, the park has a 2.5-mile paved bike path through its grasslands and

The plentiful antique windmills seen on the Livermore Winery Ride remind us that there is still plenty of "country" left in Livermore.

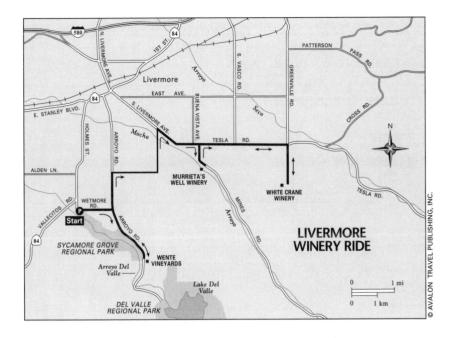

groves of sycamores. An out-and-back will add an easy, pleasant five miles to your day.

The route directions below show only the mileage along the main roads from winery to winery. Each time you choose to stop at one of the wineries, your mileage will increase as you ride up and down its driveway. I'm assuming you won't stop to wine taste at every winery mentioned (if you did, your bike handling skills would be severely compromised), so adjust your mileage according to your chosen stops. And if you want to shorten the ride, skip the out-and-back to Wente Vineyards on Arroyo Road (at .7 mile) and save 3.5 miles. Just go left on Arroyo Road instead.

If you can arrange it, try to get tickets in advance for one of the outdoor summer concerts at Livermore's Wente Vineyards (925/456-2424). You can ride all afternoon, have dinner at a restaurant in town, and go to a show in the evening. Concerts are held from June to September each year and feature well known acts like Lyle Lovett and Chris Isaak.

Have fun. And don't forget to drink some water with that wine.

Driving Directions

From I-580 in Livermore, take the North Livermore Avenue exit and turn south. Drive one mile through downtown Livermore. Turn right on Stanley Boulevard (Highway 84), then left on Holmes Street. Follow Holmes

Street for about two miles, then turn left on East Vallecitos Road (signed for the Veterans Hospital), which becomes Wetmore Road. Turn right into Sycamore Grove Park in .3 mile.

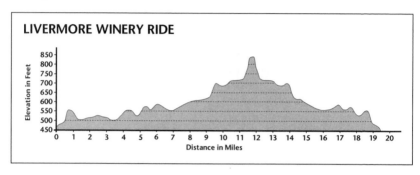

Route Directions for Livermore Winery Ride

0.0 Park at Sycamore Grove Park, then ride out to Wetmore Road and turn RIGHT. *Supplies are available in Livermore and at several wineries along the route.*

0.3 Livermore Valley Cellars.

0.7 RIGHT on Arroyo Road.

2.5 Wente Vineyards, Golf Course, Restaurant, and Visitor Center. TURN AROUND.

4.2 STRAIGHT at junction of Wetmore and Arroyo Roads.

5.0 RIGHT on Marina Avenue. Watch for speed "humps" (not bumps!).

6.0 LEFT on Wente Street.

6.5 RIGHT on Concannon Boulevard.

6.9 RIGHT on South Livermore Avenue, which becomes Tesla Road.

7.6 Concannon Vineyard.

7.9 RIGHT on Mines Road.

8.2 Murrieta's Well Winery. TURN AROUND.

8.5 RIGHT on Tesla Road.

8.8 Steven Kent Winery.

8.9 Wente Estate Vineyards (different from Wente Vineyards).

9.6 Rios-Lovell Winery.

10.1 Cedar Mountain Winery.

10.5 Garre Vineyard and Café.

10.6 RIGHT on Greenville Road.

11.1 Poppy Ridge Golf Course.

11.6 Bent Creek Winery.

11.7 White Crane Vineyards. TURN AROUND.

13.0 LEFT on Tesla Road.

16.1 LEFT on Concannon Boulevard.

16.5 LEFT on Wente Street.

17.0 RIGHT on Marina Avenue.

18.0 LEFT on Arroyo Road.

18.8 RIGHT on Wetmore Road.

19.5 Arrive at starting point.

40. ALAMEDA CREEK TRAIL

Fremont to Coyote Hills Regional Park

Type of trail: paved bike path

Difficulty: *I □ □ □ □*   **Total distance:** 24 miles (or longer options)

Riding time: 2 hours   **Elevation gain:** 200 feet

Alameda Creek, the largest stream in Alameda County, was once a valuable resource to the Ohlone Indians who settled along its banks. Today, Alameda Creek Trail follows the creek from the mouth of Niles Canyon in Fremont 12 miles westward to San Francisco Bay.

The trail is actually two parallel trails on the south and north bank of the creek. The south-side trail (paved) is for bikers, hikers, and runners, and the north side (unpaved) is for equestrians, too. The south-side trail, described here, accesses Coyote Hills Regional Park, where more riding is available.

Everything is in place here to make your ride easy. Unlike some trails in the East Bay's impressive system of paved recreation paths, the Alameda Creek Trail is unique in that it is uninterrupted by street intersections, so

Don't forget your binoculars for birdwatching when you ride the Alameda Creek Trail to Coyote Hills Regional Park.

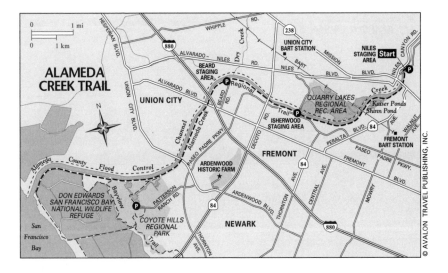

you have 12 miles of worry-free riding in both directions. Mileage markers are installed along the trail, and water and restrooms are available at several points. Even when the afternoon westerly wind comes up from the bay, it will be at your back for the slightly uphill ride home.

Alameda Creek Trail passes under highway overpasses and alongside neighborhood backyards, so it isn't exactly a nature trail, although you will probably spot birds along the narrow-channeled creek. If you're clamoring for something more, well, natural, add on a ride in Coyote Hills Regional Park, a bayside park with an abundance of wildlife and fascinating Native American history. Skinny-tire riders are restricted to adding 3.5 paved miles on the park's Bay View Trail, but mountain bikers can pedal around on the numerous dirt trails that roll up and down Coyote's rounded hills. Those who enjoy steep ups and fast downs should not miss Red Hill Trail, but the park has many other trail options for mountain bikers.

For more information, contact East Bay Regional Park District, 510/635-0135 or 510/562-7275, website: www.ebparks.org.

Driving Directions
From I-680 in Fremont, take the Mission Boulevard exit and drive northwest for four miles to Highway 84/Niles Canyon Road. Turn right, then right again on Old Canyon Road. The staging area is on the left.

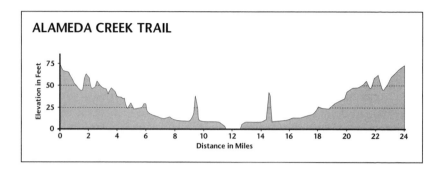

ALAMEDA CREEK TRAIL

Route Directions for Alameda Creek Trail

0.0 Park at Niles staging area and follow the trail out of the parking lot. *Water and restrooms are available at the staging area and along the trail.*

1.4 Pass Kaiser and Shinn Ponds.

2.6 Bridge at end of Thornton Avenue.

3.5 Isherwood Staging Area.

4.3 Decoto Road.

5.4 End of Beard Road; Beard Staging Area.

6.1 I-880.

6.4 Alvarado Boulevard.

7.8 Newark Boulevard.

9.7 Sign at base of hill leading to Coyote Hills Regional Park.

12.0 Edge of San Francisco Bay. TURN AROUND. *Or, take the 50-foot connector trail from Alameda Creek Trail to the paved Bayview Trail in Coyote Hills Regional Park, adding on a 3.5-mile paved loop. Mountain bikers can add on several miles of dirt riding in the park.*

24.0 Arrive at starting point.

© ANN MARIE BROWN

Chapter 3

South Bay and the Peninsula

41. SWEENEY RIDGE LOOP

Golden Gate National Recreation Area near Pacifica

Type of trail: dirt road and paved roads with moderate car traffic

Difficulty: 💧💧💧🔘🔘

Total distance: 7.3 miles

Riding time: 2 hours

Elevation gain: 1,100 feet

It's steep, it's fast, and it's well-loved by Pacifica locals. The Sweeney Ridge Loop is the perfect length for a good bout of exercise and it can be completed in a couple of hours. Better still, on clear days it offers one of the best views in the Bay Area, an incredible 360-degree panorama from the top of Sweeney Ridge. This vista takes in the Pacific coastline and San Francisco Bay as well as the land mass to the east, north, and south—including Montara Mountain, Mount Tamalpais, Mount Diablo, Mount Hamilton, Point Reyes, Point San Pedro, and the Farallon Islands. But remember, clear days are rare in Pacifica, especially in summer. If you want to see the view, ride here in one of the other seasons.

This loop route isn't for the aerobically challenged. It starts out with a serious climb on Mori Ridge Trail, an old dirt road, gaining 700 feet in 1.3

Mountain bikers, hikers, and dog walkers enjoy the view from the top of Sweeney Ridge.

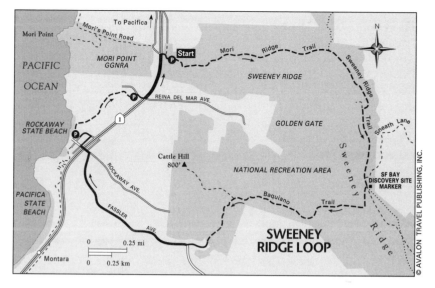

miles. There is no warm-up; you just get into your lowest gear at the trailhead and crank uphill. The trail leads through open grasslands and coastal
scrub, with occasional Monterey pines presenting a chance for shade. When
Mori Ridge Trail meets up with Sweeney Ridge Trail, the aerobic challenge is
over. Turn right for a much easier cruise to an old Nike missile site, then follow the paved trail south from the decaying military buildings to the San
Francisco Bay Discovery Site. It was here, at the 1,220-foot summit on top of
Sweeney Ridge, that Gaspar de Portolá first sighted San Francisco Bay on No-
vember 4, 1769. A stone monument commemorates the discovery.

You're back on dirt now and ready to start your descent on Baquiano
Trail. The trail gets steeper and faster as it goes, so watch your speed. Remember: Hikers and dog walkers also use this trail, and they don't appreciate getting run over by bikes. You'll drop down to a gate at the end of
Fassler Avenue in Pacifica, then continue steeply downhill to Highway 1,
now on pavement and in the company of car traffic. Cross to the west
side of the highway at Rockaway Avenue, pick up the short but scenic
bike path alongside Calera Creek, then cross Highway 1 again at Reina del
Mar Avenue. The last stretch back to your car is, unfortunately, the least
pleasant of the trip: a .3-mile stint on the wide Highway 1 shoulder, then
a steep .3-mile stint up the driveway to Shelldance Nursery and back to
the trailhead. But the rest of the loop makes it worth it.

For more information, contact Golden Gate National Recreation Area
Presidio Visitor Center, 415/561-4323, or the Fort Funston Ranger Station,
415/239-2366. Website: www.nps.gov/goga.

Driving Directions

From Highway 1 in Pacifica, turn east into the driveway for Shell Dance Nursery (north of Reina del Mar Avenue and south of Sharp Park Road). Drive .3 mile, past the nursery buildings, to the signed Sweeney Ridge Trailhead parking area. (If you are driving south on Highway 1, you will have to make a U-turn and head north to enter the Shell Dance Nursery driveway.)

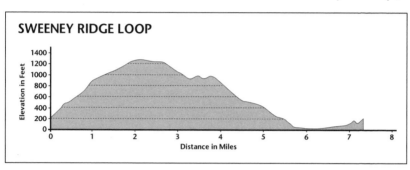

SWEENEY RIDGE LOOP

Route Directions for Sweeney Ridge Loop

0.0 Park at the Sweeney Ridge Trailhead by Shell Dance Nursery. Begin riding on the trail heading uphill from the trailhead sign. *Supplies are available in Pacifica.*

1.3 RIGHT at junction of Mori Ridge Trail and Sweeney Ridge Trail.

2.1 Nike missile site; dirt trail meets up with paved trail along the ridge top; follow paved trail.

2.6 STRAIGHT on dirt trail where pavement turns sharply left.

2.7 RIGHT on Baquiano Trail at San Francisco Bay Discovery Site marker.

4.0 Go through gate.

4.1 LEFT at trail fork.

4.4 Pass water tank; trail becomes old paved road.

4.5 Go through gate at end of Fassler Avenue; watch for cars on downhill.

5.8 Cross Highway 1 to Rockaway Beach Avenue.

5.9 RIGHT on Dondee Way.

6.0 LEFT on San Marlo Way.

6.1 Parking lot by beach; pick up paved bike trail on right side of parking lot.

6.6 Bike trail ends at parking lot by Reina del Mar Avenue; ride out to Highway 1 and cross it.

6.7 LEFT on Highway 1; ride north using wide shoulder, passing police station.

7.0 RIGHT at Shell Dance Nursery driveway; steep uphill.

7.3 Arrive at starting point.

42. MONTARA MOUNTAIN

McNee Ranch State Park north of Half Moon Bay

Type of trail:  dirt road and deteriorating pavement

Difficulty: 𝗜 𝗜 𝗜 𝐼 𝐼

Total distance: 9.6 miles

Riding time: 2 hours

Elevation gain: 2,000 feet

This view of the treacherous stretch of coast known as Devil's Slide is a good reason for a rest stop on the ascent up Montara Mountain.

You like a long, sustained hill climb and a lightning-fast descent? You get them both on this ride from the Pacific Ocean to the top of Montara Mountain, elevation 1,898 feet. Make sure your body has plenty of fuel and water for the 4.8-mile climb up, and wear your sturdiest helmet for the ride down.

Aside from the heart- and leg-pumping work, there isn't much to think about on this ride, which has almost no intersections. Instead, you can focus on the views, which are downright spectacular on clear days. You ride with the ocean mostly at your back for the first 1.5 miles, heading deep into Montara Mountain's coastal canyon. Gradually the trail rises above the valleys and starts to show off glimpses of the blue Pacific. At the 2.2-mile mark, where two posts mark a side trail off-limits to bikes,

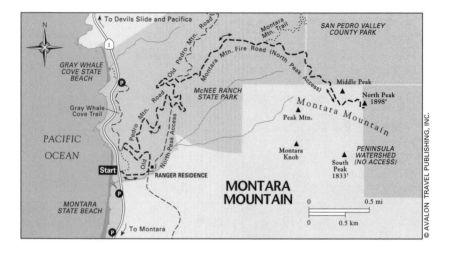

the panorama opens wide, exposing the crashing surf and tall cliffs of
Montara State Beach (650/726-8819) and Gray Whale Cove. From this
point onward, every time you pause to catch your breath those sublime
ocean vistas are waiting for you.

When at last you attain Montara Mountain's transmitter tower–littered
summit, your view expands to include the north and east: Mount Tamalpais, the skyline of San Francisco, the famous sign on U.S. 101 proclaim-
ing "South San Francisco the Industrial City," San Mateo Bridge, San
Francisco Bay, plus Mount Diablo in the background. This is one of the
most all-encompassing views possible in the Bay Area.

The trail's grade is fairly moderate all the way up except for one .5-mile
stretch at 2.6 miles, which is *really* steep (it gains 500 feet in .5 mile). The
path's first 2.4 miles are a mix of deteriorating pavement, gravel, and dirt
(often squeezed into single-track by encroaching pampas grass). You're riding
on old San Pedro Mountain Road, which used to be the route from Montara to
Pacifica before Highway 1 was built. The last 2.4 miles follow Montara Mountain Fire Road, a wide dirt road. Because of its rough surface, descending can
be like riding on ball bearings; it's difficult to control your speed. Move your
butt way back off your seat or you'll go down for sure. Guess how I know?

Driving Directions

From Half Moon Bay, drive north on Highway 1 for 10 miles to just north
of Montara State Beach and the Chart House Restaurant and just south of
Devil's Slide. The trailhead is marked by a yellow metal gate on the east
side of the highway, with parking for about six cars. If this lot is full, park
.2 mile farther south at Montara State Beach.

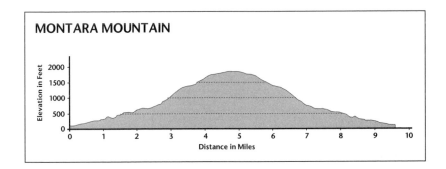

MONTARA MOUNTAIN

Route Directions for Montara Mountain

0.0 Park at McNee Ranch trailhead by the yellow metal gate. Begin riding on the wide road behind the gate (not the single-track trail). *Supplies are available in Montara, one mile south.*

0.2 LEFT at fork by ranger's house.

1.7 Dirt road merges in from the right.

2.2 Coastal viewpoint where hiker's trail leads west (signed as "No Bikes").

2.4 RIGHT on dirt Montara Mountain Fire Road (deteriorating pavement veers to the left); prepare for brutal .5-mile climb.

3.5 Pass Montara Mountain Trail on left (hikers-only trail from San Pedro Valley County Park).

4.4 South Peak of Montara Mountain on left; continue straight.

4.8 Arrive at North Peak of Montara Mountain. TURN AROUND. *Climb up the rocky, short trail (about 20 feet) next to the communication towers for the best view of the day.*

9.6 Arrive at starting point.

43. SAWYER CAMP RECREATION TRAIL

Crystal Springs Reservoir near Hillsborough and Millbrae

Type of trail:  paved bike path

Difficulty: 𝐼 𝟙 𝟙 𝟙

Total distance: 12 miles

Riding time: 1 hour

Elevation gain: 250 feet

Few bike trails are as well-loved and well-used as the Sawyer Camp Trail. This paved, car-free recreation trail is long enough so you can feel like you got some exercise riding it, easy enough so that even the most casual rider can try it, and surprisingly scenic as well. Its only drawback is its popularity: With so many people living nearby on the northern Peninsula, the trail is almost always packed with walkers, runners, in-line skaters, and baby strollers, in addition to bikers. No matter; just get here early to avoid the crowds, especially on weekends.

The trail travels the length of Lower Crystal Springs Reservoir, then leads through marshlands to southern San Andreas Lake, ending just beyond the lake's dam at Hillcrest Boulevard in Millbrae. Unlike many paved recreation trails, it isn't as straight as a stick; it twists and curves

Cyclists share Sawyer Camp Trail's six mile length with joggers and other users.

gracefully around the reservoir's shoreline. You have a good chance of seeing deer, raptors, herons, and egrets somewhere along the route.

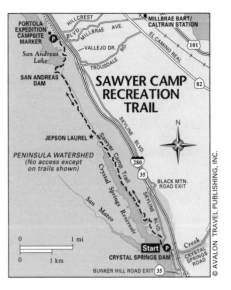

The ride is an easy cruise; you probably won't even shift gears for the first 4.5 miles. The only noticeable hill is in the last stretch near San Andreas Lake's dam. Be sure to make a stop to see the Jepson laurel tree, 3.5 miles in and 25 feet off the trail (near a picnic area). More than 600 years old and 55 feet tall, the tree is the oldest and largest living California laurel, named for botanist Willis Jepson.

Another of the trail's highlights is a plaque on a boulder at trail's end at Hillcrest Boulevard, which marks the spot where Captain Gaspar de Portolá made camp after his discovery of San Francisco Bay in 1769.

Riders looking for more mileage can connect this trail with a ride on Cañada Road, two miles south of the Sawyer Camp Trailhead, which is good for riding any time but especially good every Sunday, when four miles of its length are closed to cars. For more information on Cañada Road Bicycle Sunday, phone San Mateo County Parks and Recreation, 650/363-4020.

Driving Directions

From I-280 in San Mateo, take the Highway 92 exit west, then turn right (north) immediately on Highway 35. Drive .5 mile to Crystal Springs Road and the trail entrance.

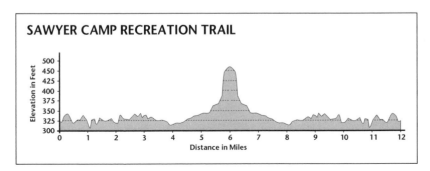

Route Directions for Sawyer Camp Recreation Trail

0.0 Park in the small parking lot by the trailhead, or alongside the road. Ride through the signed gate to enter the trail. *Water is available along the trail.*

3.5 Restrooms, drinking water, and picnic area by short path to Jepson laurel tree.

4.8 Beginning of hill climb.

5.1 Cross dam over San Andreas Lake.

6.0 Arrive at gate at Hillcrest Boulevard. TURN AROUND. *Note historic marker for Gaspar de Portolá's camp just past the gate.*

12.0 Arrive at starting point.

44. HALF MOON BAY BACK ROADS

south of Half Moon Bay

Type of trail:  paved roads with minimal car traffic

Difficulty: ▮▮▮▯▯

Riding time: 2 hours

Total distance: 24.1 miles

Elevation gain: 1,500 feet

Many Bay Area residents complain that the coastal resort town of Half Moon Bay has left its "country" roots behind and become too much of a city. This loop ride on Half Moon Bay's back roads (with a mere 6.8-mile stretch on busy Highway 1) proves that there's still plenty of country left in this coastal town; you just have to know where to find it.

The ride begins at the Half Moon Bay firehouse at the junction of Main Street and Higgins Purisima Road. The toughest part is the first 100 yards, in which you must use impeccable judgment when crossing the stream of cars on Highway 1. With this accomplished, you face a quick, level jaunt south on the highway, followed by another careful crossing and a left turn on Tunitas Creek Road. Now you're in the country, and you'll face nothing but quiet roads and pastoral scenery for the rest of your ride.

The only serious hill appears at mile 19.8, when Purisima Creek Road becomes Higgins Purisima Road at a hairpin turn in the road. Here you'll gain 400 feet in about two miles, then lose it again on your way back into town. Otherwise, there's some climbing on Lobitos Creek Road, but it's nothing to complain about. The views of the remote coastal canyons will more than compensate.

Driving Directions

From Half Moon Bay at the junction of Highway 92 and Highway 1, head south on Highway 1 for 1.2 miles to Higgins Purisima Road (by the firehouse). Turn left and park along Main Street near the firehouse.

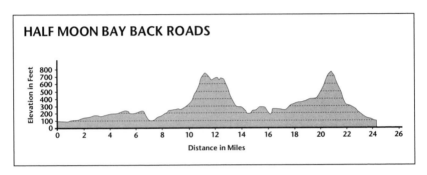

HALF MOON BAY BACK ROADS

Route Directions for Half Moon Bay Back Roads

0.0 Park on the south end of Main Street in Half Moon Bay, near its junction with Higgins Purisima Road and Highway 1. Ride out the last few yards of Higgins Purisima Road and cross Highway 1 to head south. *Supplies are available on Main Street or Highway 1 in Half Moon Bay.*

1.9 Pass Cowell Ranch Beach turnoff.

6.8 LEFT on Tunitas Creek Road.

8.8 RIGHT at junction with Lobitos Creek Cutoff.

9.8 Enter redwoods.

10.4 LEFT on Lobitos Creek Road (a very sharp left turn).

14.6 RIGHT on Verde Road (parallels Highway 1 with nice views of the ocean).

16.2 RIGHT on Purisima Creek Road.

19.8 Pass entrance to Purisima Creek Redwoods Open Space Preserve at hairpin turn; road changes names to Higgins Purisima Road.

24.1 Arrive at starting point.

45. PURISIMA REDWOODS LOOP

off Skyline Boulevard near Woodside

Type of trail: dirt road and single-track; paved road with moderate car traffic

Difficulty: ❚❚❚❘❘

Riding time: 2–3 hours

Total distance: 10 miles

Elevation gain: 1,600 feet

It might seem more sensible to start this loop ride from its lowest point, at the Purisima trailhead south of Half Moon Bay, so that you could climb uphill when you're fresh and save the downhill for the way home. But there's room for only a few cars at the Half Moon Bay trailhead, and these spaces are almost always filled. Unless you live in or near Half Moon Bay, it's not worth the drive to the trailhead only to discover there is no place to park.

Instead, start this ride at the top of the loop, at the large Purisima parking lot on Skyline Boulevard near Woodside. Folks who live in San Francisco and the northern Peninsula will find that this trailhead is close enough that they can show up after work on the long days of summer and still have enough daylight to complete the ride.

"Summer" is a key word here, because the Whittemore Gulch section of this trail is closed to bikes during the rainy season. It's a beautiful single-track trail

The single-track Whittemore Gulch Trail is a favorite route of mountain bikers in Purisima Creek Redwoods Open Space Preserve.

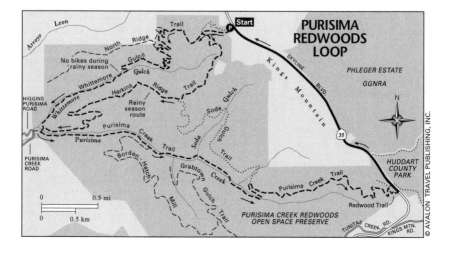

tunneling through a flower-filled Douglas fir forest, with lots of fun twists and tight turns. (You access it .8 mile from the trailhead, after a rather bumpy ride on North Ridge Trail, a dirt road.)

The upper section of Whittemore Gulch Trail provides long-distance views of the Half Moon Bay coast—or Half Moon Bay fog, depending on the weather. The trail keeps descending until, at about two miles from the start, you enter a deep, dark redwood canyon. The area was logged in the late 1800s, so these are second- and third-growth trees, but impressive nonetheless. The return leg of the loop is uphill on Purisima Creek Trail, a gradual but steady climb alongside a pretty stream and some very large redwoods, followed by a quick, two-mile stint on paved Skyline Boulevard.

If you must ride in the wet season, you can follow an alternate route in Purisima from the same trailhead: downhill on Harkins Ridge Trail and uphill on Purisima Creek Trail. The Midpeninsula Regional Open Space District (650/691-1200, website: www.openspace.org) keeps these wide trails open no matter what the weather. There's no comparison, though; Whittemore Gulch is the trail to ride in this park.

Driving Directions

From San Francisco, drive south on I-280 for 19 miles to the Highway 92 west exit. Go west on Highway 92 for 2.7 miles, then turn left (south) on Highway 35 (Skyline Boulevard). Drive 4.3 miles to the Purisima Creek Redwoods Open Space Preserve parking area on the right.

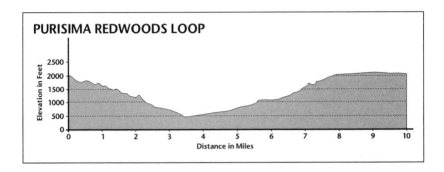

PURISIMA REDWOODS LOOP

Route Directions for Purisima Redwoods Loop

0.0 Park at Purisima parking lot on Skyline Boulevard. Follow North Ridge Trail (dirt road) from the parking lot (not the hikers-only trail). *Supplies are available eight miles south on Skyline Boulevard at Skylonda.*

0.3 Straight at junction with Harkins Ridge Trail.

0.8 LEFT on Whittemore Gulch Trail.

1.4 LEFT to stay on Whittemore Gulch Trail.

2.8 Cross footbridge; trail widens and levels out.

3.7 STRAIGHT at junction with Harkins Ridge Trail. Cross wide bridge ahead.

3.8 LEFT on Purisima Creek Trail on far side of bridge.

4.8 STRAIGHT at junction with Borden Hatch Mill Trail.

5.1 STRAIGHT at junction with Grabtown Gulch Trail.

6.1 RIGHT at junction with Soda Gulch/Bay Area Ridge Trail.

7.8 RIGHT on Redwood Trail.

8.0 LEFT on Skyline Boulevard.

10.0 Arrive at starting point.

46. EL CORTE DE MADERA CREEK LOOP

off Skyline Boulevard near Woodside

Type of trail:  dirt road and single-track

Difficulty: ▮▮▮◌◌

Total distance: 10.5 miles

Riding time: 2 hours

Elevation gain: 1,400 feet

Of all the beautiful open space lands on Skyline Boulevard, El Corte de Madera Creek Open Space Preserve is the one most favored by mountain bikers. Partly it's because almost every trail is open to bikes, and partly it's because so many of those trails are single-track. To sweeten the pot, the trail is densely shaded with second- and third-growth redwoods, making it a good choice for warm summer days when you want to ride where you won't bake in the sun.

The loop described below is designed to string together an abundance of single-track, but that means you have to put up with a lot of trail directions. One thing this preserve has plenty of, besides redwood trees, is junctions. It's common to see riders stopped at intersections here—they're usually consulting a map, or each other.

This loop is also designed to keep you away from the many hikers who walk the short trail to the preserve's main attraction, a tafoni sandstone formation. Except for a brief stretch where your paths may in-

Almost every trail at El Corte de Madera Creek Open Space Preserve, including plentiful stretches of single-track, is open to mountain bikers.

© ANN MARIE BROWN

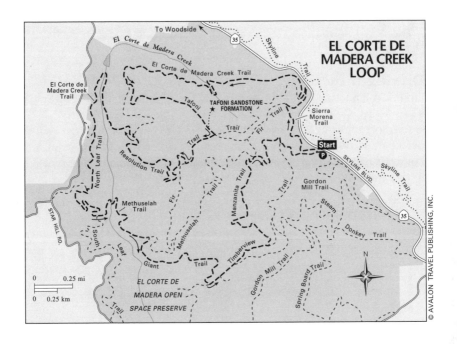

tersect, you should be far from the vast majority of pedestrians on this loop. Don't forget to bring a bike lock so your can chain up your wheels and walk the short path to see this cluster of 50-foot-high sandstone outcrops. Tafoni is a type of sandstone that is formed by years of weathering. The "glue" that holds the sandstone's individual sand grains together slowly erodes away, leaving honeycomb patterned, lace-like crevices and holes in the smooth rock. From an observation deck at the end of this .2-mile trail, you have a good vantage point for gazing in awe at the tafoni. Just don't think about riding your bike on this trail; it's for hiking only.

Another attraction this loop visits is the Old Growth Redwood, the only one left standing in this preserve. The tree is noticeably larger than its hundreds of second- and third-growth compatriots at El Corte de Madera Creek.

But mostly it's the riding you'll enjoy here. Highlights include the too-short romps on Giant Salamander and North Leaf Trails and a challenging climb on Resolution Trail (all single-track). Note that many of the trails are quite steep (even the single-tracks), so if you don't enjoy a lot of ups and downs, you won't be happy here. Overall, this is not a place for beginners to ride because of technical challenges, but intermediates will have a great time on the frequent sharp corners, steep ascents and descents, tree roots, and rocky and loose trail surfaces.

For more information, contact the Midpeninsula Regional Open Space District, 650/691-1200, website: www.openspace.org.

Driving Directions

From San Francisco, drive south on I-280 for 19 miles to the Highway 92 west exit. Go west on Highway 92 for 2.7 miles, then turn left (south) on Highway 35 (Skyline Boulevard). Drive 8.9 miles to the trail-head parking on the west side of the road, .4 mile south of Skeggs Vista Point. (If this small lot is full, park at the vista point lot and ride south to this trailhead.)

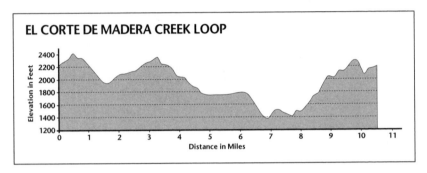

EL CORTE DE MADERA CREEK LOOP

Route Directions for El Corte de Madera Creek Loop

0.0 Park at the CM02 gate and ride to your right (north) on Sierra Morena Trail. *Supplies are available in Skylonda, 3.4 miles south on Skyline Boulevard.*

0.6 RIGHT on Fir Trail.

0.8 Gate at Skyline Boulevard; turn sharply LEFT on Tafoni Trail.

0.9 RIGHT on El Corte de Madera Creek Trail.

1.6 LEFT to stay on El Corte de Madera Creek Trail (turns to single-track).

2.4 LEFT on Tafoni Trail.

3.2 Hiker's trail to tafoni sandstone formation on left. *Lock up your bike and walk the .2-mile trail to the see the tafoni.*

3.3 RIGHT (sharp) on Fir Trail at four-way junction.

3.5 LEFT at Vista Point Trail to stay on Fir Trail.

3.6 RIGHT on Resolution Trail (single-track).

4.7 LEFT on El Corte de Madera Creek Trail.

5.2 Cross El Corte de Madera Creek.

5.6 LEFT on North Leaf Trail (single-track).

6.7 LEFT on Methusaleh Trail (single-track).

6.8 Cross El Corte de Madera Creek.

7.1 RIGHT on Giant Salamander Trail (single-track).

8.0 LEFT on Timberview Trail.

8.1 Old Growth Redwood. *Pay homage to the big tree.*

8.6 LEFT on Manzanita Trail (single-track).

9.7 RIGHT on Methusaleh Trail at four-way junction.

10.1 LEFT to stay on Methusaleh Trail.

10.5 Arrive at starting point.

47. WOODSIDE TO SKYLINE SHORT LOOP

Woodside to Skylonda

Type of trail:  paved roads with moderate car traffic

Difficulty: 🍶🍶🍶🍶🍶

Total distance: 20 miles

Riding time: 1.5–2 hours

Elevation gain: 2,200 feet

The Woodside to Skyline Short Loop is as close to a perfect 20-mile training ride as you can get. It has a killer 3.4-mile hill (Old La Honda Road from Woodside to Skyline Boulevard) and just enough mileage to keep your heart rate up for an hour or two. Yet it's remarkably scenic, supplies plenty of convenient places to stop for fuel or rest, and offers a mix of wide bike lanes and less-traveled country roads. You'll have to put up with some traffic on Skyline Boulevard, but the payoff is worth it. (If you want more mileage and more hills in the Woodside area, see Ride 48.)

First, know that the tony community of Woodside is Bike Central. There isn't a more bike-friendly town anywhere in the Bay Area, a region filled with bike-friendly towns. And there isn't a more likely place to spot

The historic Woodside Store (now a museum) is filled with local history.

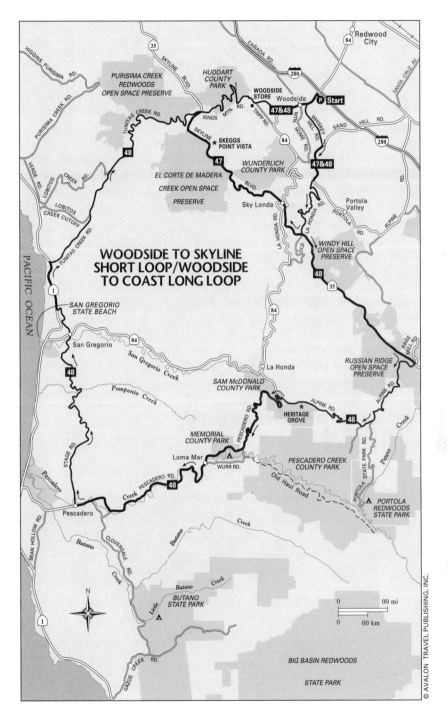

the most expensive bikes, the hottest gear, and the tautest leg muscles. It seems that people who can afford to live in Woodside have plenty of time for recreation and fitness. You can't hold it against them.

Whiskey Hill and Sand Hill Roads both have wide bike lanes that will get you through the busy Woodside corridor. Then you begin your epic climb on extremely narrow Old La Honda Road, a former logging toll road that today twists and turns through second- and third-growth redwoods. On any weekend day you'll find members of local cycling clubs racing each other up this one-lane hill. Fortunately, few car drivers use Old La Honda Road except for those who live on it. It's so steep and narrow that at its high terminus on Skyline Boulevard it is signed "Downhill Bicycling Not Recommended."

The climb continues, more gradually now and with one 400-foot dip, as you cruise north on Skyline Boulevard. You can stop in Skylonda for a cool drink, or just continue onward to your big descent on Kings Mountain Road. Then it's back to Woodside, passing Huddart Park and the historic Woodside Store along the way. Stop in if it's open; the old store is now a museum with fascinating artifacts from the area's pioneer past.

Driving Directions
From I-280, take the Highway 84/Woodside exit and drive west for less than .25 mile to the Park and Ride lot.

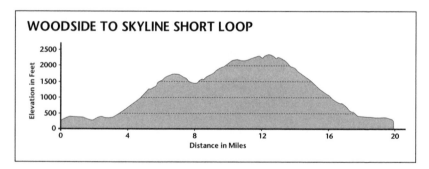

WOODSIDE TO SKYLINE SHORT LOOP

Route Directions for Woodside to Skyline Short Loop

0.0 Park at the Woodside Park and Ride lot. Ride west on Woodside Road (Highway 84). *Supplies are available in Woodside.*

0.5 LEFT on Whiskey Hill Road.

1.8 RIGHT on Sand Hill Road at Y-junction.

3.2 RIGHT on Old La Honda Road.

6.6 RIGHT on Skyline Boulevard.

8.1 Skylonda market and Alice's Restaurant at junction of Skyline and Highway 84. *Supplies are available.*

11.9 Skeggs Vista Point on right.

13.6 RIGHT on Kings Mountain Road.

16.5 Entrance to Huddart Park on left. *Water is available.*

17.7 LEFT at stop sign at Entrance Way.

17.9 Historic Woodside store at Tripp Road junction. *Stop in to the museum to see the local history exhibits.*

18.6 LEFT on Woodside Road (Highway 84).

19.4 Downtown Woodside. *Supplies are available.*

19.5 STRAIGHT at junction with Whiskey Hill Road (start of loop).

20.0 Arrive at starting point.

48. WOODSIDE TO COAST LONG LOOP

Woodside to Pescadero

Type of trail:  paved roads with moderate car traffic

Difficulty: 𝕴𝕴𝕴𝕴𝕴

Total distance: 57.1 miles

Riding time: 5–7 hours

Elevation gain: 4,900 feet

For trail map, see page 167 (Ride 47: Woodside to Skyline Short Loop)

A lot of hill climbing and a lot of scenery make up this all-day ride from Woodside to the coast. With 4,900 feet of elevation gain, it's not for the faint of heart. But for an epic cycling adventure in the San Francisco Bay Area, this loop can't be beat.

The ride's first 6.6 miles mimic those of the Woodside Short Loop, Ride 47 in this chapter. But where riders on the short loop head north on Skyline Boulevard, you'll head south, passing by Windy Hill and Russian Ridge Open Space Preserves while gaining another 500 feet, then turn west on Alpine Road. I hope your brakes are in good working order, because you're going to descend 2,000 feet in the next seven miles. Most of

A cycling club gathers on Skyline Boulevard after the climb from Woodside.

it is in open grasslands, but you also pass through a stretch of old-growth redwoods, called the Heritage Grove, in Alpine Road's last two miles. Lock up your bike and take a short walk through these magnificent trees.

With a left turn on Pescadero Road, you'll climb again over a steep grade for almost two miles, which seems like a terrible injustice. But then you drop again, this time all the way to sea level in the town of Pescadero. After a food and rest break in this small village, Old Stage Road and Highway 1 take you over comparatively easy terrain (two 300-foot climbs) to Tunitas Creek Road, where you begin your last major climb of the day. This nine-miler is one of the favorite training rides of cyclists on the coast. Why? Three reasons: The majority of it is in shady redwoods, the climb holds an average six percent grade (total 2,000-foot gain), and cars are a rarity. On nice weekends, the road is lined with dozens of cyclists.

Did I mention that the last six miles from Skyline Boulevard are all downhill back to your car? And a well-deserved downhill at that.

Driving Directions
From I-280, take the Highway 84/Woodside exit and drive west for less than .25 mile to the Park and Ride lot.

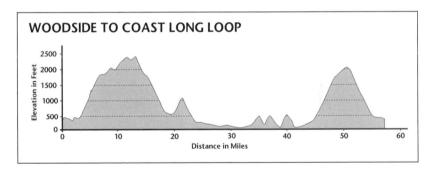

Route Directions for Woodside to Coast Long Loop

0.0 Park at the Woodside Park and Ride lot. Ride west on Woodside Road (Highway 84). *Supplies are available in Woodside.*

0.5 LEFT on Whiskey Hill Road.

1.8 RIGHT on Sand Hill Road at Y-junction.

3.2 RIGHT on Old La Honda Road.

6.6 LEFT on Skyline Boulevard. *Supplies are available 1.5 miles north (right) in La Honda.*

12.2 RIGHT on Alpine Road.

15.6 RIGHT to stay on Alpine Road.

15.9 RIGHT to stay on Alpine Road.

18.4 Small parking area and hiking trail at Heritage Grove.

19.7 LEFT on Pescadero Road.

20.2 Entrance to Sam McDonald County Park. *Water is available.*

24.1 Entrance to Memorial County Park. *Water is available.*

25.4 Loma Mar Store. *Supplies are available.*

31.5 RIGHT on Stage Road in Pescadero. *Supplies are available in Pescadero.*

38.7 Cross Highway 84 and stay on Stage Road. *Supplies are available at San Gregorio Store.*

39.8 RIGHT on Highway 1.

41.4 RIGHT on Tunitas Creek Road.

43.4 RIGHT at junction with Lobitos Creek Cutoff.

45.0 RIGHT at junction with Lobitos Creek Road.

50.5 Cross Skyline Boulevard and continue on Kings Mountain Road.

53.6 Entrance to Huddart Park on left. *Water is available.*

54.8 LEFT at stop sign at Entrance Way.

55.7 LEFT on Woodside Road (Highway 84).

56.5 Downtown Woodside. *Supplies are available.*

56.6 STRAIGHT at junction with Whiskey Hill Road.

57.1 Arrive at starting point.

49. RUSSIAN RIDGE & COAL CREEK LOOP

off Skyline Boulevard near Palo Alto

Type of trail:  dirt road and single-track

Difficulty: ❙❙ 🚲🚲🚲

Total distance: 7.3 miles

Riding time: 1.5 hours

Elevation gain: 800 feet

Russian Ridge is one of the few open space preserves on Skyline Boulevard where beginning mountain bikers have a chance to ride without becoming discouraged by the technical nature of the trails. Conveniently, it's also more than 1,500 acres of windswept ridge-top paradise, which will charm you in every season of the year. In summer and fall, the hillsides turn gold and the grasses sway in unison to the ridge-top winds. In winter, the trunks of the moss-covered oaks and laurels turn a bright verdant green. And in spring, the grasslands explode in a fireworks display of colorful mule's ears, poppies, lupine, goldfields, johnny jump-ups, and blue-eyed grass.

This loop route combines a ride through Russian Ridge Open Space Preserve with a ride through neighboring Coal Creek Open Space Preserve,

Russian Ridge Open Space Preserve offers easy to moderate trail riding through grasslands and spring wildflowers.

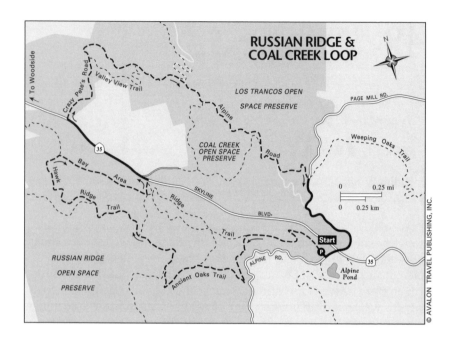

directly across Skyline Boulevard. You'll get to try out your skills on mostly wide fire roads, with a few stints on manageable single-track. This loop is a great place to become more confident on two wheels, and at the same time enjoy some beautiful scenery. If you feel like you're getting in over your head at any point, don't be afraid to dismount your bike and walk.

Although each stretch of this loop has its own rewards, a few trails deserve special mention. Ancient Oaks Trail in Russian Ridge is a single-track that leads through a remarkable forest of gnarled, moss-covered oak trees interspersed with equally gnarled Douglas firs, plus some madrones and ferns. You may want to linger a while in this strange, enchanted woodland. The route follows a historic road in Coal Creek Open Space Preserve—the old Alpine Road on the east side of Skyline Boulevard, which was closed to cars in the late 1960s. The road was originally built by San Mateo County as a way of encouraging commerce from Santa Cruz County, while simultaneously bypassing Santa Clara County. (Alpine Road on the west side of Skyline is still open to cars.) The stretch that is covered in this loop—from Crazy Pete's Road to Page Mill Road—looks much more like a trail than a road. It's fun to imagine cars negotiating its narrow turns.

For more information, contact the Midpeninsula Regional Open Space District, 650/691-1200, website: www.openspace.org.

Driving Directions

From I-280 in Palo Alto, take the Page Mill Road exit west. Drive 8.9 winding miles to Skyline Boulevard (Highway 35). Cross Skyline Boulevard to Alpine Road. Drive 200 feet on Alpine Road and turn right into the Russian Ridge entrance.

Or, from the junction of highways 35 and 9 at Saratoga Gap, drive seven miles north on Highway 35 (Skyline Boulevard). Turn left on Alpine Road and then right into the preserve entrance.

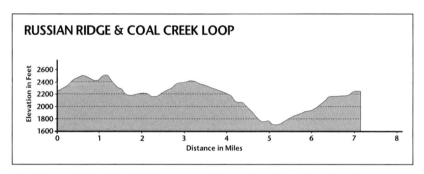

RUSSIAN RIDGE & COAL CREEK LOOP

Route Directions for Russian Ridge & Coal Creek Loop

0.0 Park at the Russian Ridge main trailhead at Alpine Road and Skyline Boulevard. Ride north on Bay Area Ridge Trail (near restroom). *Supplies are available in Skylonda, 7.5 miles north on Skyline Boulevard.*

0.5 LEFT on connector trail to Ancient Oaks Trail.

0.8 RIGHT on Ancient Oaks Trail.

1.6 RIGHT on Mindego Ridge Trail (wide road).

1.9 STRAIGHT at junction.

2.1 RIGHT on Hawk Trail.

2.7 RIGHT on Bay Area Ridge Trail.

3.2 LEFT to ride out to Skyline Boulevard.

3.3 LEFT (north) on Skyline Boulevard.

4.0 RIGHT on Crazy Pete's Road.

4.4 RIGHT at junction (go through gate).

5.1 RIGHT at junction to stay on Crazy Pete's Road.

5.4 RIGHT on old Alpine Road.

6.5 RIGHT on Page Mill Road (paved road).

7.1 Cross Skyline Boulevard to Alpine Road.

7.2 RIGHT into trailhead parking area.

7.3 Arrive at starting point.

50. STANFORD & PORTOLA VALLEY LOOP

Palo Alto to Portola Valley

Type of trail:  paved roads with moderate car traffic

Difficulty: 🍶🍶🍶🍶🍶

Riding time: 1.5 hours

Total distance: 18 miles

Elevation gain: 750 feet

This road ride is more urban than many others in this book, yet it covers some of the most bicycled territory in the Peninsula, the site of millions of "after-work" or "in-between-classes" rides. The Loop, as it's known, is the kind of route where you'll find cyclists at any hour of any day, working off a little stress from their high-tech jobs or harried Stanford studies. If you choose to ride your mountain bike here, you can take off from the paved roads onto dirt trails in Arastradero Preserve and/or Windy Hill Open Space Preserve.

Cyclists start this ride from all over the Stanford and Palo Alto area; for convenience, I've written it to begin at the Stanford Shopping Center. If you feel daunted by the first stint on busy Sand Hill Road's bike lane, fear

The popular Alpine Inn is a cyclist's landmark on the Stanford & Portola Valley Loop.

not; you'll also ride a much quieter stretch on Portola Road and Alpine Road.

In addition, I've added to the traditional Loop a peaceful, two-mile, country-lane stretch on Arastradero Road, passing the grassy hills of Arastradero Preserve. This out-and-back begins at the historic Alpine Inn, formerly Rossotti's or "Zot's," reputed to be the oldest

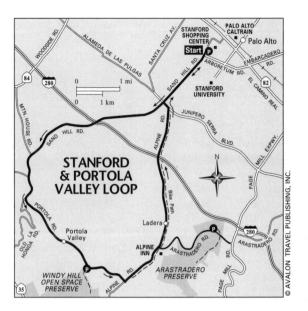

roadhouse in continuous operation in California. In the late 1800s, officials at Stanford tried to have the drinking and gambling establishment shut down, fearing its bad influence on students. They didn't succeed, and of course, the Alpine Inn has been a popular Stanford beer-and-burger hangout ever since.

When you ride through the pleasant, small town of Portola Valley, you might want to stop to see the little red Portola schoolhouse next to the town hall and library. Built in 1909, it now serves as an art gallery. The dirt trails of Windy Hill Open Space Preserve are also accessible from the roadside parking lot in Portola Valley (mile 7.6).

On the return leg on Alpine Road, you can opt to pick up the recreation trail that runs alongside the road, starting just past Los Trancos Road. The paved surface is a bit rough, however, so many cyclists stick to the wide shoulder of Alpine Road.

Driving Directions
From I-280 in Woodside, take the Sand Hill Road exit and drive east 2.8 miles to Arboretum Road and the Stanford Shopping Center.

STANFORD & PORTOLA VALLEY LOOP

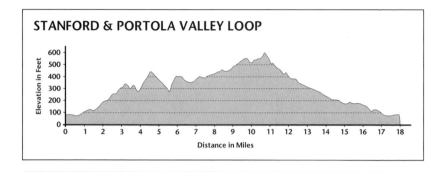

Route Directions for Stanford & Portola Valley Loop

0.0 Park at the Stanford Shopping Center near the junction of Arboretum Road and Sand Hill Road (near Nordstrom's). Ride west on the Sand Hill Road bike lane. *Supplies are available in Stanford Shopping Center.*

2.8 Cross under I-280.

5.1 Sand Hill Road becomes Portola Road (stay straight).

7.6 Parking area on right for Windy Hill Open Space Preserve in Portola Valley. *Mountain bikers can ride trails here.*

8.4 LEFT on Alpine Road. *Café and stores available at this junction.*

9.5 RIGHT on Arastradero Road; the Alpine Inn is immediately on the right. *Food and drinks are available at Alpine Inn.*

10.9 Arastradero Preserve on left (main entrance). *Mountain bikers can ride trails here.*

11.5 Arastradero Road ends at Page Mill Road. TURN AROUND.

13.5 RIGHT on Alpine Road (back at Alpine Inn).

15.3 Cross under I-280.

16.5 STRAIGHT at stoplight on to Santa Cruz Avenue.

16.6 RIGHT on Sand Hill Road.

18.0 Arrive at starting point.

51. PESCADERO & SAN GREGORIO LOOP

San Mateo County coast south of Half Moon Bay

Type of trail:  paved roads with moderate car traffic

Difficulty: ▌▌▌▢▢

Total distance: 28.7 miles

Riding time: 2 hours

Elevation gain: 1,200 feet

There's one rule about riding coastal Highway 1 south of Half Moon Bay: Ride south, not north, to avoid an often ferocious headwind. This loop around the town of Pescadero allows you to experience the best of Highway 1—heading in the direction of the prevailing winds, while riding on the ocean side of the highway in the safety of a mercifully wide shoulder. The return leg of the loop traces an inland route on mellow country lanes.

Early morning or weekday rides are recommended to avoid potentially heavy beach traffic. This loop makes a great Sunday morning ride with an early start, with time allotted for coffee or breakfast stops in the charming towns of Pescadero and San Gregorio.

Although the mileage isn't high, three long, slow hills in the first six miles of Highway 1 will give you a workout. (Two more hills await on Stage Road, plus one on Cloverdale Road.) The coastal scenery on the first half of the loop is as

Pigeon Point Lighthouse, built in 1871, is one of the highlights of the Pescadero & San Gregorio Loop.

good as it gets, with nearly non-stop views of the surging sea pounding against a rocky shoreline. A highlight is a visit to Pigeon Point Lighthouse, built in 1871 and now operated as a youth hostel. Lighthouse tours are usually available on weekends for a small fee, but you can always enjoy the views from the lighthouse grounds, and the windswept coast at neighboring Whaler's Cove.

Heading south from the lighthouse, you'll turn inland at Gazos Creek Road and enjoy a rolling ride through rural coastal hills. Pedaling north toward Pescadero, you'll pass by the entrance road to Butano State Park, a pretty redwood park with a campground and hiking trails. If you have energy to burn, it's worth a ride in for a look.

In the small town of Pescadero, historic Duarte's Restaurant is a favorite breakfast and lunch stop for cyclists, and two markets sell fresh-baked breads and other goodies. The ride concludes with a 7.2-mile stint on Stage Road, which, before Highway 1 was built, was the only route from Pescadero to San Gregorio.

Driving Directions

From Highway 1 in Half Moon Bay, drive south for 13 miles to San Gregorio State Beach, just south of the junction with Highway 84. Park in the state beach parking lot.

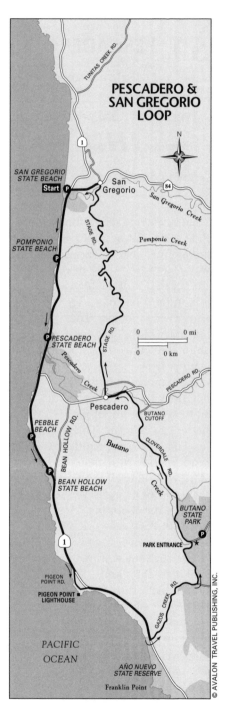

PESCADERO & SAN GREGORIO LOOP

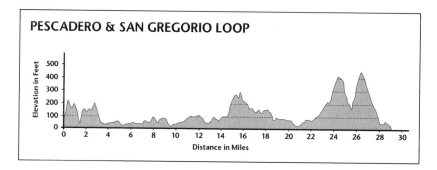

PESCADERO & SAN GREGORIO LOOP

Route Directions for Pescadero & San Gregorio Loop

0.0 Park at San Gregorio State Beach and turn right out of the lot, heading south on Highway 1. *Supplies are available in Half Moon Bay, 13 miles north on Highway 1, or in San Gregorio, .75 mile east on Highway 84.*

1.6 Pomponio State Beach.

3.5 Pescadero State Beach and Pescadero Marsh.

4.5 STRAIGHT at junction with Pescadero Road.

6.1 Pebble Beach.

7.0 Bean Hollow State Beach.

9.4 RIGHT on Pigeon Point Road; seaside riding on a quiet access road.

10.1 Pigeon Point Lighthouse. *Lighthouse tours are sometimes available on weekends.*

10.3 RIGHT on Highway 1.

12.5 LEFT on Gazos Creek Road. *Supplies are available at store 50 yards south on Highway 1.*

14.6 LEFT on Cloverdale Road.

15.8 Butano State Park turnoff on the right.

20.1 LEFT on Pescadero Road.

20.6 RIGHT on Stage Road. *Supplies are available in Pescadero (two blocks of shops).*

27.8 LEFT on La Honda Road. *Supplies are available at San Gregorio Store, straight ahead at intersection.*

28.5 LEFT on Highway 1.

28.7 Arrive at starting point.

52. OLD HAUL ROAD

Pescadero Creek County Park, Loma Mar
52A (Out-and-Back)

Type of trail: dirt road

Difficulty: 🥾🥾🥾🥾🥾   **Total distance:** 10 miles

Riding time: 1 hour   **Elevation gain:** 500 feet

52B (Old Haul Road and Alpine Road Loop)

Type of trail: dirt road and paved roads with minimal car traffic

Difficulty: 🥾🥾🥾🥾🥾   **Total distance:** 17.6 miles

Riding time: 3 hours   **Elevation gain:** 2,100 feet

The Old Haul Road is an old logging route that runs for five miles between Pescadero Creek County Park and Portola Redwoods State Park. It tunnels through a thick forest of second-growth redwoods, providing a smooth dirt route that is ideal for beginning mountain bike riders. Built on a railroad bed, it gains only 500 feet in elevation and has an easy grade in both directions. This makes the Old Haul Road a perfect choice for a carefree 10 miles of out-and-back riding.

On the Pescadero Creek County Park side, the trail starts by a small picnic area near the rushing creek gorge, then heads east. You'll see plenty of big stumps along the route—reminders of this forest's earlier state—and many tiny streams that run

© ANN MARIE BROWN

Mountain bikers can ride an easy out-and-back on Old Haul Road or a more strenuous loop.

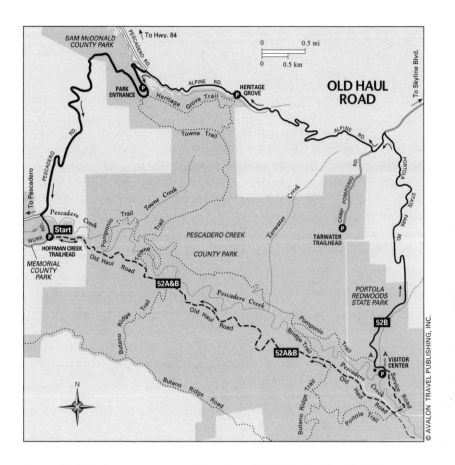

down the hillsides to empty into Pescadero Creek. The hard-packed dirt-and-gravel road is well signed and easy to follow the whole way. Your only concern is to watch out for equestrians and hikers, who also use this trail.

Those who want a more strenuous ride with greater variety can use the Old Haul Road to connect to paved Portola State Park Road and Alpine Road, home of the awe-inspiring Heritage Grove of old-growth redwoods. This loop features a long, slow climb of 900 feet over four miles on Portola State Park Road. It's followed by a long, fast descent on Alpine Road to the Heritage Grove. After enjoying the mighty trees, you face a second climb, this time with a steeper grade, as Pescadero Road ascends mercilessly for just under two miles. (Prepare to use your granny gear.) The last two miles are an easy downhill cruise back to your car. Although the roads on this loop are quite narrow, they get little traffic, so you won't have to worry much about cars.

For more information, contact San Mateo County Parks and Recreation, 650/363-4020, or Portola Redwoods State Park, 650/948-9098.

Driving Directions

From Highway 1, 15 miles south of Half Moon Bay, drive east on Pescadero Road for 9.8 miles. Turn right at the second entrance to Wurr Road, .25 mile past the entrance to Memorial Park. Drive .25 mile to the Hoffman Creek Trailhead, where Old Haul Road begins. (Or, from I-280 at Woodside, take Highway 84 west for 13 miles to La Honda. Turn left on Pescadero Road and drive one mile, then bear right to stay on Pescadero Road. Continue 4.2 miles to Wurr Road on the left. Turn left and drive .25 mile to the trailhead.)

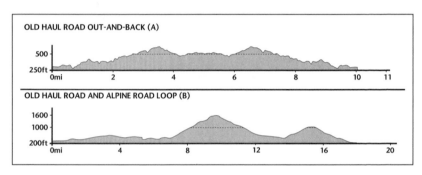

Route Directions for Old Haul Road 52A (Out-and-Back)

0.0 Park at the Wurr Road entrance to Pescadero Creek County Park. Begin riding at the entrance gate. *Supplies are available at the Loma Mar Store, 1.5 miles west on Pescadero Road.*

0.5 STRAIGHT at junction with Pomponio Trail.

1.1 STRAIGHT at junction with Towne Trail.

3.2 Reach high point in the trail and start to descend.

3.9 STRAIGHT at junction with Bridge Trail on left and Butano Ridge Trail on right.

5.0 Service road to Portola State Park on left and Portola Trail on right. TURN AROUND. *Water is available in the park.*

10.0 Arrive at starting point.

Route Directions for 52B (Old Haul Road and Alpine Road Loop)

Follow directions for Ride 52A to mile 5.0, then continue:

5.0 LEFT at service road to Portola State Park; descend and continue past the gate onto paved road.

6.0 Portola State Park visitor center and restrooms on the left. *Water is available.*

6.4 Exit out of Portola State Park and follow Portola State Park Road.

9.3 LEFT on Alpine Road.

9.6 RIGHT to stay on Alpine Road.

12.1 Heritage Grove. *Take a short walk through these magnificent trees.*

13.3 LEFT on Pescadero Road.

13.8 Entrance to Sam McDonald County Park. *Water is available.*

17.4 LEFT on Wurr Road.

17.6 Arrive at starting point.

53. BIG BASIN & BOULDER CREEK LOOP

Santa Cruz Mountains and Big Basin
Redwoods State Park

Type of trail:  paved roads with moderate car traffic

Difficulty: 𝌆𝌆𝌆𝌆𝌆   **Total distance:** 43 miles

Riding time: 3–4 hours   **Elevation gain:** 3,300 feet

This road ride explores the ridges and forests of the Santa Cruz Mountains and includes a visit to California's first state park, Big Basin Redwoods. You'll see plenty of redwoods along the route, plus ridgeline forests of madrone and oak. Long climbs and descents are part of the package, and you'll have to put up with auto traffic on narrow, shoulderless roads. But it's worth it to complete this 43-mile epic trip through some of the South Bay's most remote countryside.

The loop ride begins at Saratoga Gap at the junction of Highway 9 and Skyline Boulevard and heads southwest to Big Basin Redwoods State Park (831/338-8860 or 831/429-2851). A six-mile descent from Saratoga Gap at 2,634 feet to Waterman Gap at 1,267 feet is your warm-up for the day. Continuing straight on narrow, twisting Highway 236, you'll face a moderate up-and-down ride to state park headquarters. Lock up your bike at the parking lot and take the .5-mile walk on Redwood Trail, which shows

This shoulderless stretch of Highway 9 leads to Big Basin Redwoods State Park.

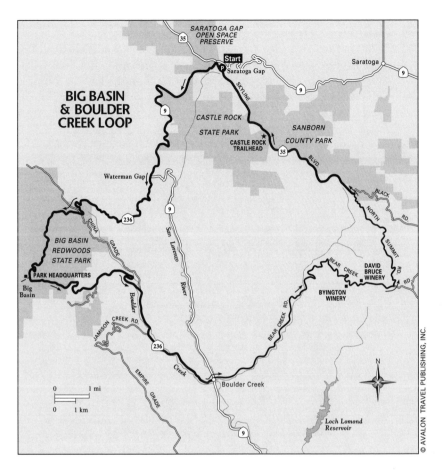

BIG BASIN & BOULDER CREEK LOOP

off some of the park's largest and oldest redwoods, including the Mother of the Forest (329 feet tall) and the Santa Clara Tree (17 feet in diameter). Nothing compares to the humbling feeling of walking in the shadows of 2,000-year-old giants.

Back on your bike, you'll exit the park and continue south on Highway 236, climbing briefly and then dropping down to the town of Boulder Creek. After a food and rest stop, and maybe a triple espresso, you face a strenuous climb from Boulder Creek (500 feet in elevation) to North Summit Road near Los Gatos (2,200 feet in elevation). You'll pass two wineries along the way. If you can somehow pull yourself through this unforgiving stretch, the remaining miles on narrow North Summit Road and Skyline Boulevard will seem relatively easy. Thankfully, the last two miles on Skyline Boulevard to your car at Saratoga Gap are actually downhill.

Driving Directions

From I-280 in Palo Alto, take Page Mill Road west for 8.9 miles to Skyline Boulevard (Highway 35). Turn left (south) on Skyline and drive 10.5 miles to the junction with Highway 9. The parking lot is on the left. Or, from Saratoga, take Highway 9 west for 7.5 miles to its junction with Skyline Boulevard (Highway 35).

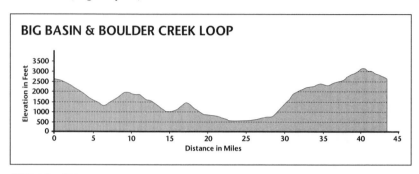

BIG BASIN & BOULDER CREEK LOOP

Route Directions for Big Basin & Boulder Creek Loop

0.0 Park at the large parking lot at the junction of Highway 9 and Highway 35. Ride west on Highway 9. *A vendor sells hot dogs and drinks in the parking lot on most weekends. Other supplies are available in Saratoga.*

1.8 Overlook point and restrooms on left.

6.1 RIGHT on Highway 236 at Waterman Gap.

10.8 STRAIGHT at junction with China Grade.

14.2 Big Basin Redwoods State Park headquarters. *Lock up your bike and take a hike on the .5-mile Redwood Trail from the main parking lot. Water, restrooms, and a small store are available (open most of the year).*

20.6 Pass golf course.

23.5 LEFT onto Highway 9 at stop sign. *Supplies are available in town of Boulder Creek.*

23.6 RIGHT on Bear Creek Road.

28.3 Begin major climb.

31.0 Byington Winery on right.

31.6 David Bruce Winery on left.

32.6 LEFT on North Summit Road (unsigned except for spray-painted word "Skyline" and arrow); end of major climb.

36.5 STRAIGHT at junction with Black Road; North Summit Road widens and becomes Skyline Boulevard.

40.4 Castle Rock State Park entrance.

43.0 Arrive at starting point.

54. SARATOGA GAP LOOP

off Skyline Boulevard near Saratoga

Type of trail: dirt road and single-track

Difficulty: ▮▮▮◊◊

Total distance: 12.9 miles

Riding time: 2–3 hours

Elevation gain: 1,600 feet

When I was first getting into mountain biking, I met a pro rider on the trail who gave me one piece of advice: "If you want to learn how to handle single-track, ride Saratoga Gap Trail—often."

It was sage advice. I'm still not the world's greatest single-track rider (not even close), but I know where to go to sharpen my skills.

So does everyone else. This loop is one of the most popular in the South Bay, and for good reason. It starts at the busy junction of Highways 9 and 35, with easy access from most of Silicon Valley and the Peninsula, and carves its way through three separate parks and preserves: Saratoga Gap, Long Ridge, and Upper Stevens Creek.

© ANN MARIE BROWN

This ride through Long Ridge Open Space Preserve is one of the easier stretches of the Saratoga Gap Loop.

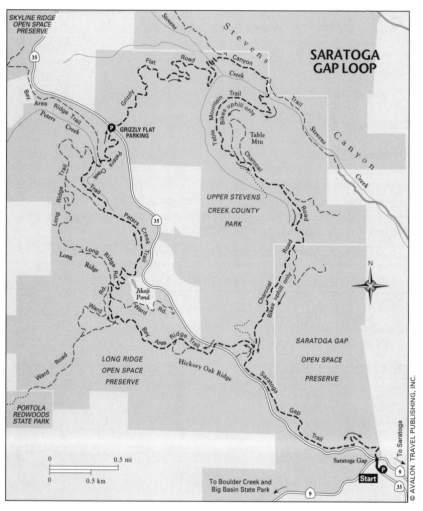

The loop can be ridden in only one direction because one leg is open to uphill traffic only. If you can take your eyes off the six-foot space in front of your front tire, you'll find that the surrounding foothill scenery is lovely: open grassland ridges, fern-filled forests of handsome Douglas firs, wide views of wooded hillsides, and even a visit to a trickling creek in Stevens Canyon, which makes a perfect mid-loop rest stop.

Aside from the technical challenges of single-track on Saratoga Gap, Peters Creek, and Table Mountain trails, the only major difficulty on this ride is the long climb out on Charcoal Road, a 1.5-mile workout. But since it is preceded by a steep descent on Grizzly Flats Trail to Stevens

Canyon, you are clearly forewarned that the uphill is coming. More than a few riders have been spotted walking their bikes here.

Note that this is a dry-season-only loop; many of the trails are closed during wet weather. Please don't ride them illegally.

For more information, contact Midpeninsula Regional Open Space District, 650/691-1200, website: www.openspace.org.

Driving Directions

From I-280 in Palo Alto, take Page Mill Road west for 8.9 miles to Skyline Boulevard (Highway 35). Turn left (south) on Skyline and drive 10.5 miles to the junction with Highway 9. The parking lot is on the left. Or, from Saratoga, take Highway 9 west for 7.5 miles to its junction with Skyline Boulevard (Highway 35).

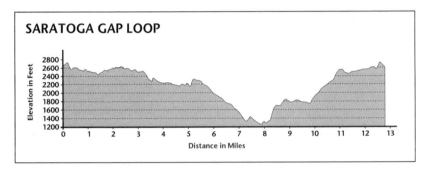

Route Directions for Saratoga Gap Loop

0.0 Park at the large parking lot at the junction of Highway 9 and Highway 35. Ride across Highway 9 carefully to access Saratoga Gap Trail. *A vendor sells hot dogs and drinks in the parking lot on most weekends. Other supplies are available in Saratoga.*

2.0 Single-track Saratoga Gap Trail ends at Highway 35; cross the highway and go RIGHT on Bay Area Ridge Trail.

3.2 RIGHT on single-track (signed for Grizzly Flat parking).

3.3 STRAIGHT at junction with Ward Road on left.

3.4 RIGHT on single-track Peters Creek Trail at major junction of Ward Road, Long Ridge Road, and Peters Creek Trail.

4.3 RIGHT to stay on Peters Creek Trail. Keep to right at next two forks to come out to Highway 35.

5.3 Cross Highway 35 and pick up Grizzly Flat Road on other side; steep and long descent.

7.8 Cross Stevens Creek.

8.0 RIGHT on Canyon Trail.

8.3 RIGHT on Table Mountain Trail (single-track signed "To Saratoga Gap").

9.5 RIGHT on Table Mountain Trail/Charcoal Road (wide road).

9.9 RIGHT on Charcoal Road; begin major hill climb.

10.4 RIGHT to stay on Charcoal Road.

11.2 LEFT at junction with Saratoga Gap Trail. *There are Miwok Indian grinding stones near this junction.*

12.9 Arrive at starting point.

55. SARATOGA TO MONTEBELLO ROAD SUMMIT

Saratoga to Montebello Ridge
55A (Paved Out-and-Back)

Type of trail: paved roads with moderate car traffic

Difficulty: 𝍠𝍠𝍠 𝍠𝍠　　　　　　**Total distance:** 21.2 miles

Riding time: 2 hours　　　　　　　**Elevation gain:** 2,000 feet

Ride 55B (Paved and Dirt Loop)

Type of trail dirt road and single-track;

　　　　　　　　　　　paved roads with moderate car traffic

Difficulty: 𝍠𝍠𝍠𝍠 𝍠　　　　　　**Total distance:** 27 miles

Riding time: 3 hours　　　　　　　**Elevation gain:** 2,300 feet

The roads around Stevens Creek Reservoir and throughout Stevens Creek Canyon are well traveled by cyclists from the Silicon Valley every day of the week. The nearness of this pretty, tree-lined canyon to the hustle and bustle of Cupertino makes it perfect for after-work, lunchtime, and weekend rides.

The two rides described here, one entirely paved and one a combination of pavement and dirt, are designed to allow for the most scenery with the least traffic. Both routes travel up Pierce Road from Saratoga through a mix of vineyards, red-tile-roofed mansions, and older farmhouses, then cruise through the foothills of Mount Eden Road and creek-side Stevens Canyon Road to Montebello Road. Following this route, you've encountered two brief climbs already, but from here on out there's nothing but climbing on Montebello's increasingly narrow road. The road gains 1,500 feet over 4.3 miles, with grades occasionally as steep as 13 percent.

Achieving Montebello's high ridge is your reward, with its spreading views overlooking the Santa Clara Valley and a chance for wine tasting and a picnic at Ridge Winery (weekends only). The paved road continues a mile beyond Ridge Winery, but the views don't get much better. On the

Bikes of all shapes and sizes can be ridden to the summit of Montebello Road.

way back downhill, you may be able to stop at the Pichetti Ranch and Winery for some live music (Sunday only).

Mountain bikers have another option (Ride 55B). From Ridge Winery, continue up Montebello Road to the Waterwheel Creek Trail in Montebello Open Space Preserve, then follow that trail to the dirt section of Montebello Road. Shortly, you're at the microwave-covered summit of 2,800-foot Black Mountain, the highest point on Montebello Ridge. Views are good in all directions, but the best view is to the west, as seen from near the 15-mph speed limit sign at an obvious outcrop of scattered rocks: Stevens Creek Canyon lies below you. Untrammeled grassland hills spread to the north and south along Skyline Ridge. The Pacific Ocean glimmers from afar. In springtime, the grassland wildflowers explode in a riot of colors.

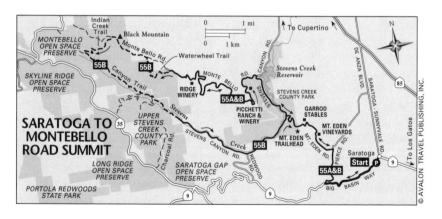

The all-dirt downhill is exciting and fast; be careful not to mow over cyclists riding in the opposite direction. Indian Creek Trail drops 850 feet over 1.2 miles, then Canyon Trail descends almost as fast, adding a little single-track to the mix. Where the dirt ends, you follow paved Stevens Canyon Road to Mount Eden Road, then retrace your tracks to Saratoga.

For more information, contact Midpeninsula Regional Open Space District, 650/691-1200, website: www.openspace.org.

Driving Directions

From San Jose, take Highway 17 south for six miles to the Highway 9 exit in Los Gatos. Take Highway 9 northwest 2.5 miles into Saratoga and park in downtown.

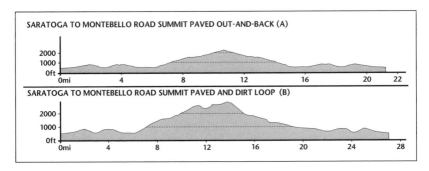

Route Directions Ride for Saratoga to Montebello Road Summit 55A (Paved Out-and-Back)

0.0 Park in downtown Saratoga in any of the public parking lots one block off Highway 9. Ride west on Highway 9. *Supplies are available in town.*

1.6 RIGHT on Pierce Road (signed for Mountain Winery).

2.6 LEFT on Mount Eden Road.

3.1 Mount Eden Vineyards.

3.5 Garrod Farm Stables.

4.1 Mount Eden Trailhead on the left (no bikes).

4.9 STRAIGHT on Stevens Canyon Road at stop sign.

6.3 LEFT on Montebello Road.

6.8 Pichetti Ranch and Winery at Montebello Open Space Preserve (live music on Sunday).

8.3 Road narrows considerably.

10.6 Ridge Winery on the left. TURN AROUND. *Wine-tasting on weekends; restrooms and water are available.*

21.2 Arrive at starting point.

Route Directions Ride 55B (Paved and Dirt Loop)

Follow Ride 55A to mile 10.6 (Ridge Winery), then continue up Montebello Road:

11.5 LEFT on Waterwheel Creek Trail (gated dirt trail).

12.9 LEFT on Montebello Road (dirt).

13.8 Summit of Black Mountain.

14.1 LEFT on Indian Creek Trail.

15.0 LEFT on Canyon Trail, stay left at next two junctions to stay on Canyon Trail.

18.5 Gate and start of Stevens Canyon Road.

20.4 LEFT to stay on Stevens Canyon Road.

22.1 RIGHT on Mount Eden Road.

27.0 Return to starting point.

56. COYOTE CREEK TRAIL

San Jose to Morgan Hill

Type of trail: 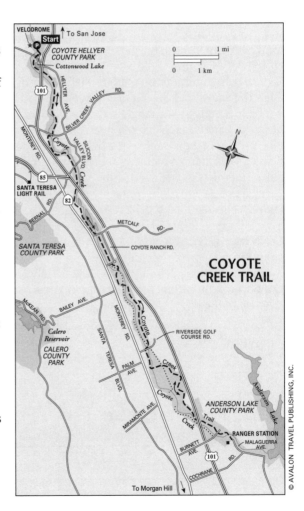 paved bike path

Difficulty: 〖〗〗〗〗

Riding time: 2–3 hours

Total distance: 29.4 miles

Elevation gain: 400 feet

Think San Jose and you probably think "industrial parks." It's true, San Jose has more than its share of these mammoth concrete complexes, but it also has peaceful farmlands, orchards, and gurgling creeks. The Coyote Creek Trail passes by all of these on its 14.7-mile length from Coyote Hellyer County Park south to Anderson Lake County Park. This makes a level, 29.4-mile round-trip on a paved recreation trail. If you simply want to crank out some level miles on your bike without worrying about cars or trail junctions, this is a good place to do it, and it's close to home for millions of Bay Area residents.

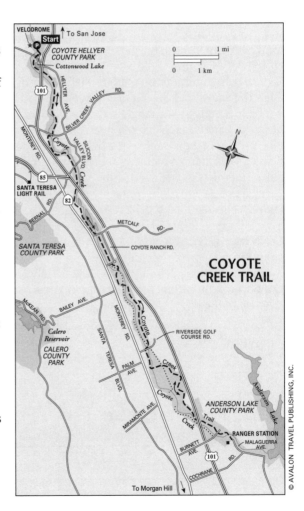

The trail begins at Coyote Hellyer County Park (408/225-0225), home of the only velodrome in Northern California. Bike races are usually held on Friday nights in summer. The open-air velodrome was built in 1962 as a training site for the Pan American Games.

In the trail's first half mile, you'll ride past small Cottonwood Lake on the left, a popular spot with shore fishermen. The lake, which was developed out of an old rock quarry, is stocked with rainbow trout. Shortly beyond it, the trail crosses under U.S. 101 to the highway's east side. You'll cross the highway twice more along the route.

As you ride, ignore the numerous side bridges over Coyote Creek that access San Jose neighborhoods. Stay on the main path, which for a paved trail is a bit rough in places. You'll have to put up with the steady hum of road noise from U.S. 101 and Monterey Highway, which are never far away. But you'll also have the fine companionship of shady sycamores, cottonwoods, and live oaks along Coyote Creek, plus occasional scrub jays and ground squirrels. South of Metcalf Road, an equestrian trail parallels the paved trail, so you may see some horses, too.

The trail ends by the ranger station at Anderson Lake County Park, site of Santa Clara County's largest reservoir. You might want to lock up your bike here and take a walk on the one-mile, self-guided nature trail that runs to Malaguerra Avenue. It, too, follows Coyote Creek; a printed trail guide interprets its riparian habitat.

For more information, contact Santa Clara County Parks and Recreation Department, 408/355-2200.

Driving Directions

From San Jose, drive four miles south on U.S. 101 and take the Hellyer Avenue exit. Drive .25 mile to the Coyote Hellyer County Park entrance. Just beyond the entrance kiosk, bear left at the fork and park at the velodrome parking lot.

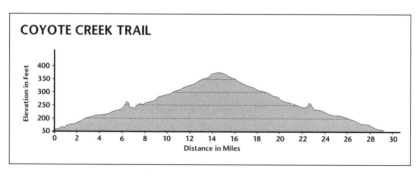

Route Directions for Coyote Creek Trail

0.0 Park at the velodrome parking lot. The bike path begins by the restrooms. *Water is available at the park.*

0.4 Cottonwood Lake on the left.

0.8 Cross under U.S. 101.

3.0 LEFT at tricky intersection on far side of bridge.

5.5 Cross under U.S. 101.

6.8 Cross Metcalf Road to Coyote Ranch Road; go right to continue on path.

7.7 LEFT on Coyote Ranch Road, then RIGHT back onto path.

10.6 Cross Riverside Golf Course road.

14.0 Cross under U.S. 101.

14.7 Arrive at the ranger station for Anderson Lake County Park. TURN AROUND. *Water is available at the park.*

29.4 Arrive at starting point.

57. MOUNT HAMILTON

Joseph D. Grant County Park, southeast of San Jose

Type of trail:  paved road with minimal car traffic

Difficulty: *IIII* **Total distance:** 23 miles (or longer options)

Riding time: 2 hours **Elevation gain:** 2,700 feet

The summit of Mount Hamilton, at 4,209 feet, is high enough so that on those rare winter days when snow falls in the Bay Area, it is gloriously crowned in white. It's the Bay Area's loftiest peak, and the highest you can drive to—or ride your bike to. It's also the home of Lick Observatory (visitor center, 408/274-5061), where astronomers from the University of California keep a watch on the stars. Constructed in 1887 by James Lick, the observatory was once famous for its 36-inch telescope, the world's largest at that time.

The ascent to Mount Hamilton's summit is challenging, but not impossibly so, thanks to the curving, twisting, switchbacking, steady 5- to 7-percent grade of Mount Hamilton Road. Beginning from Joseph D. Grant County Park (408/274-6121), you have 11.5 miles to gain 2,700 feet in elevation to the summit (this includes a 300-foot descent to Smith Creek, which you must regain).

Junctions are few and far between on this road, so you don't have route directions to worry about. Just follow the pavement uphill, through a landscape of grasslands, buckeyes, and

wild pig warning is posted on Mount Hamilton Road near the observatory mistletoe-draped oaks. In spring, the mountain is well known for its wildflower displays, and in autumn, the fall colors on the upper slopes can be delightful. As you ascend the mountain, you'll notice the foliage change: Coulter pines with their big, heavy cones appear among the manzanita, plus leafy black oaks. It gets cooler the higher you go, and the views of Santa Clara Valley get better and better.

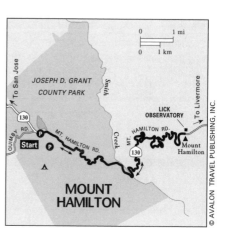

If you want to keep riding beyond the summit, help yourself. San Antonio Valley Road rolls, winds, and gradually descends until it changes names to Mines Road and eventually winds up in Livermore, 45 miles later. Almost no cars travel this stretch of road, so it's all yours. If you happen to know someone in Livermore who will give you a ride back to Joseph Grant Park, you're in for a fine day.

Driving Directions

From I-680 in San Jose, take the Alum Rock Avenue exit and drive east 2.2 miles. Turn right on Mount Hamilton Road and drive 7.8 miles to the main entrance to Joseph D. Grant County Park on the right. Park in the county park lot (fee charged) or alongside the road in pullouts (no fee).

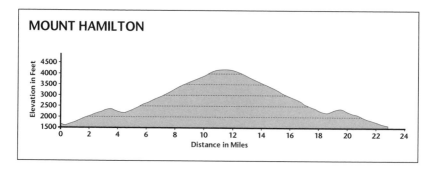

Route Directions for Mount Hamilton

0.0 Park near the entrance to Joseph D. Grant County Park and ride southeast on Mount Hamilton Road. *Water is available in the park campground; supplies are available eight miles north in San Jose.*

3.5 Twin Gates Trailhead and start of descent to Smith Creek. *Now or on the return trip, take a walk on Cañada de Pala Trail to see an abundance of blue-eyed grass, johnny jump-ups, brodiaea, shooting stars, and goldfields (springtime only).*

4.4 Smith Creek bridge.

5.6 STRAIGHT at junction with Kincaid Road on left.

10.9 RIGHT at Lick Observatory junction.

11.5 Arrive at main building and visitor area of observatory. TURN AROUND. *Water and snack machines are available when the visitor center is open, weekday afternoons and weekends 10 A.M.–5 P.M. Public tours are available.*

23.0 Arrive at starting point.

58. GRANT RANCH LOOP

Joseph D. Grant County Park, southeast of San Jose

Type of trail:  dirt road

Difficulty: ▮▮▮▯▯

Total distance: 10.9 or 12 miles

Riding time: 2 hours

Elevation gain: 1,600 feet

Joseph D. Grant County Park (408/274-6121), called "Grant Ranch" by the locals, lies due north of better known Henry Coe State Park, and it shares the same summer weather—hot as Hades. Plan your trip for the cooler months, preferably April or May when the grasslands are green and the slopes are gilded with wildflowers.

The park's trails are predominantly multiuse dirt roads that are used by mountain bikers more than anybody else. Almost every trail is an old ranch road, so if you are a single-track snob, you won't be happy here.

This challenging figure-eight loop trip takes you to the highest point in the park, Antler Point at 2,995 feet. The first two miles include some memorably steep uphill pitches, but the rest of the trip is more moderate.

At Joseph D. Grant County Park, most of the riding is on old ranch roads with steep pitches on some of the hills.

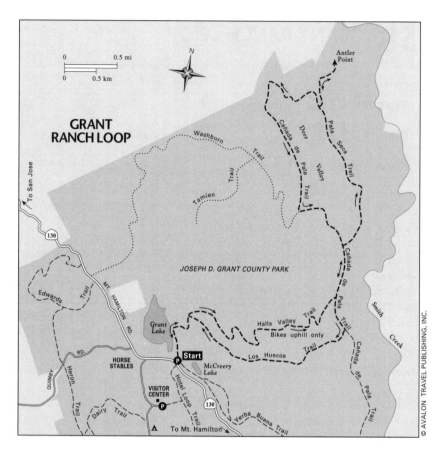

The ride starts at the Grant Lake Trailhead and follows Halls Valley Trail (open to bikes in the uphill direction only). The next 2.1 miles are the toughest of the ride, but as you gain elevation, you also gain surprising views of the South Bay's distant shimmering waters.

Where the trail tops out at Cañada de Pala Trail, turn left and enjoy an easier, more rolling grade. More views of the South Bay are seen to the northwest and Mount Hamilton shows up to the east. Look for abundant displays of spring wildflowers on this high, bald ridge.

Your destination, Antler Point, is visible straight ahead, the highest hill around. Follow Pala Seca Trail through grasslands and occasional grazing bovines to Antler Point's spur trail. This grassy overlook supplies the day's best view of the South Bay, San Jose, Grant Park's rolling grasslands, and Lick Observatory on top of 4,209-foot Mount Hamilton.

For your return trip, loop back on Cañada de Pala Trail, enjoying more high views. You have some choices for the final leg: Los Huecos Trail (a very fast and steep downhill for a 10.9-mile loop) or Yerba Buena Trail (a more gentle downhill for a 12-mile loop). The latter will get you away from the biking crowds, but if you love screaming downhills, Los Huecos Trail is the only way to go.

Driving Directions

From I-680 in San Jose, take the Alum Rock Avenue exit and drive east 2.2 miles. Turn right on Mount Hamilton Road and drive 7.8 miles to the sign for Joseph D. Grant County Park on the right. Don't turn here; continue another 100 yards to the Grant Lake parking lot on the left.

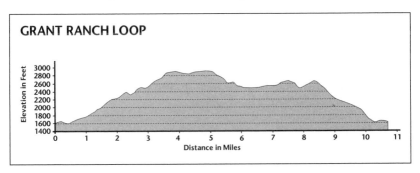

GRANT RANCH LOOP

Route Directions for Grant Ranch Loop

0.0 Park at the Grant Lake parking area. Follow the trail to the left to Grant Lake. *Water is available at the park campground.*

0.3 RIGHT on connector trail to Halls Valley Trail.

0.6 Straight on Halls Valley Trail and begin steep climb.

2.7 LEFT on Cañada de Pala Trail.

3.1 RIGHT on Pala Seca Trail.

4.8 RIGHT on Antler Point Trail (walk your bike .2 mile uphill to this 2,995-foot viewpoint).

4.9 Arrive at Antler Point. TURN AROUND.

5.1 RIGHT at junction with Pala Seca Trail.

8.1 LEFT to stay on Cañada de Pala Trail.

8.5 RIGHT on Los Huecos Trail; begin fast, steep descent. *If you prefer a gentler descent, continue on Cañada de Pala Trail for 1.3 miles farther and turn right on Yerba Buena Trail; this gets you back to your car in a 12-mile round-trip.*

10.3 STRAIGHT to return to Grant Lake.

10.6 LEFT to return to parking lot.

10.9 Arrive at starting point.

59. MIDDLE RIDGE LOOP

Henry W. Coe State Park east of Morgan Hill

Type of trail:  dirt road and single-track

Difficulty: ▌▌▌▌▐

Total distance: 10.8 miles

Riding time: 2 hours

Elevation gain: 2,100 feet

The closest thing to a wilderness park in the South Bay area is Henry W. Coe State Park (408/779-2728, website: www.coepark.parks.ca.gov). This well known but little traveled state park is the second largest in California (the largest is Anza-Borrego Desert State Park near San Diego). Composed of tall ridges bisected by deep, steep ravines, the park is notoriously hilly. Its varied terrain includes grasslands, oaks, chaparral, pines, and mixed hardwoods.

Henry Coe is so large—80,000 acres—and its terrain is so rugged that to see much of it, you need to pack your bike's panniers and plan to stay for a few days. But day visitors can tour the western part of the park on this 10.8-mile loop around Middle Ridge. The ride has some of the finest single-track to be found in the South Bay, but it also has some of the steepest fire road climbs. Come mentally and physically prepared for a workout; this park is not for beginners.

Henry W. Coe State Park provides a challenging single-track ride on the Middle Ridge Loop.

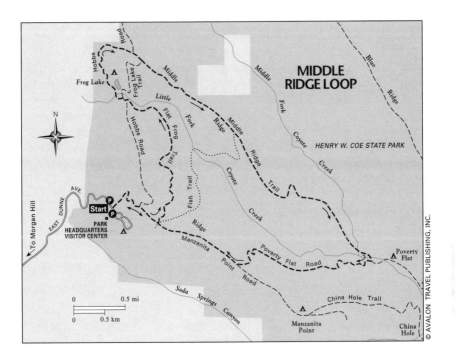

Pick a cool day for the ride, ideally in spring when Coe Park's wildflowers are blooming, or in autumn when the air is clear and cool. The park is extremely hot in summer, and its single-track trails are temporarily closed after winter rainstorms. Also in the rainy months, the wide Middle Fork of Coyote Creek at mile 7.2 may be more than a few feet deep and too dangerous to cross. Check with rangers before riding this loop after a period of rain.

The first leg of the ride follows Flat Frog Trail, a pleasant single-track that leads through a mixed woodland of ponderosa pines, black oaks, and madrones. The trail connects with Hobbs Road just before Frog Lake; take the steep ranch road to the former cattle pond. (A backpacking camp is located nearby.) Tiny Frog Lake is spring-fed; it supports a few bass and bluegill. Frequently, the surface of the water is completely covered with green algae. Cross Frog Lake's inlet and continue steeply uphill to Middle Ridge. The oak-dotted grasslands above Frog Lake support colorful wildflowers, which give you something to look at while you stop to catch your breath.

Once you reach Middle Ridge, look forward to a roller-coastering descent with many fine views of Coyote Creek canyon. Although Middle Ridge Trail initially leads through alternating grassy clearings and groves of pines and black oaks, it later enters a grove of giant, tree-sized manzanitas growing 15 feet tall. The trail loses 1,700 feet over 3.4 miles (with one short but steep uphill), and becomes more technical as it drops. In its final mile, it is downright treacherous—steep, loose, narrow, rocky, and rutted.

After crossing the Middle Fork of Coyote Creek, get ready to pay the price for all the fun you've had: You face a 1.8-mile climb on rocky Poverty Flat Road with a 1,400-foot elevation gain (12 percent average grade). Sometimes mountain biking is hell, and this is one of those times. When at last you reach Manzanita Point Road, the punishment is over, and you have an easy ride back to your car.

Driving Directions

From U.S. 101 in Morgan Hill, take the East Dunne Avenue exit and drive east for 13 miles to Henry W. Coe State Park headquarters.

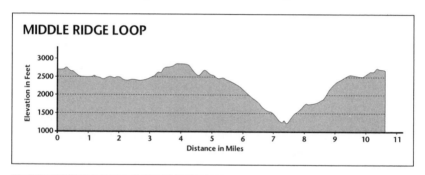

Route Directions for Middle Ridge Loop

0.0 Park at the lot near park headquarters. Follow paved Manzanita Point Road from near the headquarters building (pavement ends shortly). *Water is available at the trailhead; supplies are available in Morgan Hill.*

0.5 RIGHT to stay on Manzanita Point Road at junction with Hobbs Road.

0.7 LEFT on Flat Frog Trail.

2.9 RIGHT on Hobbs Road.

3.2 Frog Lake. Cross the dam and join trail to Middle Ridge (steep climb uphill).

3.8 RIGHT on Middle Ridge Trail; begin long, steep descent.

5.1 STRAIGHT on Middle Ridge Trail at junction with Fish Trail.

7.2 Cross Middle Fork of Coyote Creek at Poverty Flat.

7.3 RIGHT on Poverty Flat Road; begin long, steep climb out.

9.1 RIGHT on Manzanita Point Road.

10.3 LEFT to stay on Manzanita Point Road.

10.8 Arrive at starting point.

60. BERRY CREEK FALLS BIKE & HIKE (SKYLINE-TO-THE-SEA TRAIL)

Big Basin Redwoods State Park south of Pescadero

Type of trail: 🚲 dirt road and single-track

Difficulty: ▌▌▯▯▯   **Total distance:** 11.6 miles (plus 1.2-mile hike)

Riding time: 2.5 hours   **Elevation gain:** 550 feet

You can see Berry Creek Falls the hard way, by hiking 5.5 hilly miles from park headquarters at Big Basin Redwoods State Park, or you can go see Berry Creek Falls the easy way, by riding your bike 5.8 nearly level miles from the coast near Davenport, then walking the last .6 mile.

The 70-foot falls are worth seeing no matter how you get there, but if you have children in tow, or if you aren't anywhere near the Boulder Creek entrance to the park, or if you'd just rather ride than walk, the bike route is a smart choice. Riders of almost any ability can handle the wide dirt road, and the trip begins and ends at an easy-access trailhead right on Highway 1.

The trail, which is the western section of the 38-mile-long Skyline-to-the-Sea Trail, used to be even easier to ride, but a series of heavy rains in the 1990s washed parts of it into Waddell Creek, forcing one stretch to be rerouted as narrow single-track with a few ludicrously

© ANN MARIE BROWN

An easy ride through the redwoods leads to beautiful Berry Creek Falls.

tight turns. The vast majority of riders simply walk their bikes through this 100-yard stretch.

The old ranch road begins by the highway, passes by Big Basin's Rancho del Oso visitor center and a few private farms, then enters the redwoods. The entire route parallels Waddell Creek until the final walk to the falls, where the trail follows Berry Creek. Several backpacking camps are located a few yards off the route, used mostly by hikers following the entire length of Skyline-to-the-Sea Trail.

Make sure you bring a bike lock so you can secure your wheels at the bike rack and take the 15-minute hike to the waterfall (bikes aren't allowed). A bench on the viewing platform at Berry Creek Falls makes a perfect spot for lunch, if it isn't already in use by somebody else. Not surprisingly, this is a popular spot year-round. Plan a weekday trip if at all possible.

For more information, contact Big Basin Redwoods State Park at 831/338-8860 or 831/429-2851.

Driving Directions

From Half Moon Bay at the junction of Highway 92 and Highway 1, drive south on Highway 1 for 30 miles to the Rancho del Oso area of Big Basin Redwoods State Park (across from Waddell Beach, 7.5 miles north of Davenport). Park on the east side of the highway by the Rancho del Oso gate.

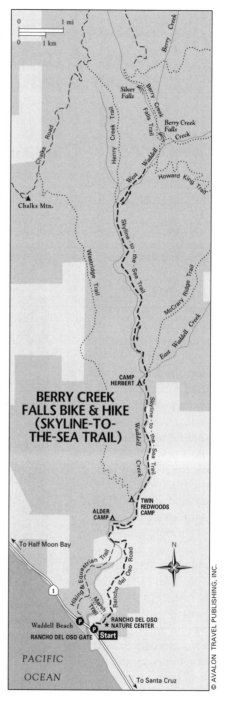

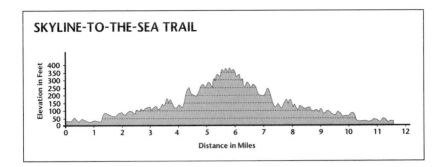

SKYLINE-TO-THE-SEA TRAIL

Elevation in Feet / Distance in Miles

Route Directions for Berry Creek Falls Bike & Hike (Skyline-to-the-Sea Trail)

0.0 Park at Rancho del Oso trailhead and ride into the parking lot and past the visitor center. *Supplies are available in Davenport, 7.5 miles south on Highway 1.*

0.4 Pass the Rancho del Oso nature center (open most weekends).

3.0 Trail washout creates tricky section with tight switchbacks. May have to walk your bike.

3.3 Cross Waddell Creek; follow the single-track trail on the right to a bridge if the stream is too high to cross.

5.8 Bike rack; TURN AROUND. *Lock up your bike and follow the hiking trail across the creek for .6 mile to Berry Creek Falls.*

11.6 Arrive at starting point.

© ANN MARIE BROWN

Resources

BIKE CLUBS IN THE
SAN FRANCISCO BAY AREA

Looking for some friends to ride with? Check out these Bay Area bike clubs:

Almaden Cycle Touring Club, San Jose
www.actc.org

Bay Area Roaming Tandems
www.bayarearoamingtandems.org

Bay Area Velo Girls
www.velogirls.com

Bicycle Trails Council of Marin
www.btcmarin.org

Bicycle Trails Council of the East Bay
www.btceastbay.org

Cherry City Cyclists, San Leandro
www.cherrycitycyclists.org

Delta Pedalers Bike Club, Antioch
www.deltaped.org

Diablo Cyclists, East Bay
www.diablocyclists.com

Different Spokes, San Francisco
www.dssf.org

Fremont Freewheelers, East Bay
www.fremontfreewheelers.org

Golden Gate Cyclists, Marin
www.goldengatecyclists.org

Grizzly Peak Cyclists, Berkeley
www.grizzlypeakcyclists.org

Marin Cyclists Road Club, Marin
www.marincyclists.com

Oakland Yellowjackets Bicycle Club, Oakland
www.oaklandyellowjackets.org

ROMP (Responsible Organized Mountain Pedalers)
www.romp.org

Tam Valley Bike Club, Marin
www.tamvalleybikeclub.com

Valley Spokesmen, East Bay
www.valleyspokesmen.org

Western Wheelers, Palo Alto
www.westernwheelers.org

Women's Mountain Bike and Tea Society (WOMBATS), Marin
www.wombats.org

SAN FRANCISCO BAY AREA BIKE SHOPS

North Bay and San Francisco

Corte Madera
REI, 213 Corte Madera Town Center, Corte Madera, 415/927-1938,
website: www.rei.com.

Fairfax
Sunshine Bicycle Center, 737 Center Boulevard, Fairfax, 415/459-3334.

Larkspur
Village Peddler, 1161 Magnolia Avenue, Larkspur, 415/461-3091, website:
www.villagepeddler.com.

Mill Valley
Mill Valley Cycleworks, 369 Miller Avenue, Mill Valley, 415/388-6774.

Novato
Bike Hut, 459 Entrada Drive, Novato, 415/883-2440.
Classcycle, 1531-B South Novato Boulevard, Novato, 415/897-3288,
website: www.classcycle.com.
Pacific Bicycle, 132 Vintage Way, Suite F13, Novato, 415/892-9319,
website: www.pacbikesandboards.com.

Petaluma
The Bicycle Factory, 110 Kentucky Street, Petaluma, 707/763-7515.
Eastside Bicycles, 701 Sonoma Mountain Parkway, Suite B-6, Petaluma, 707/766-
7501, website: www.eastsidecycles.com.
Petaluma Cyclery, 1080 Petaluma Boulevard North, Petaluma,
707/762-1990.
Sonoma Mountain Cyclery, 937 Lakeville Street, Petaluma, 707/773-3164.

Point Reyes Station
Cycle Analysis, Highway 1, Point Reyes Station, 415/663-9164, website: www.cy-
clepointreyes.com.

San Anselmo
Caesar Cyclery, 29 San Anselmo Avenue, San Anselmo, 415/721-0805.

San Francisco

American Cyclery, 858 Stanyan Street, San Francisco, 415/876-4545.

Avenue Cyclery, 756 Stanyan Street, San Francisco, 415/387-3155, website: www.avenuecyclery.com.

Big Swingin' Cycles, 1122 Taraval Street, San Francisco, 415/661-2462, website: www.bigswingincycles.com.

City Cycle of San Francisco, 3001 Steiner Street, San Francisco, 415/346-2242, website: www.citycycle.com.

DD Cycles, 4049 Balboa Street, San Francisco, 415/752-7980.

Free Wheel Bike Shop, 980 Valencia Street, San Francisco, 415/643-9213.

Fresh Air Bicycles, 1943 Divisadero Street, San Francisco, 415/563-4824.

Golden Gate Cyclery, 672 Stanyan Street, San Francisco, 415/379-3870.

Lombardi's Sports, 1600 Jackson Street, San Francisco, 415/771-0600, website: www.lombardissports.com.

Noe Valley Cyclery, 4193 24th Street, San Francisco, 415/647-0886.

Nomad Cyclery, 2555 Irving Street, San Francisco, 415/564-3568.

Ocean Cyclery, 1915 Ocean Avenue, San Francisco, 415/239-5004.

Pacific Bicycle, 345 Fourth Street, San Francisco, 415/928-8466, website: www.pacbikeonline.com.

Pedal Revolution, 3085 21st Street, San Francisco, 415/641-1264.

Road Rage Bicycles, 1063 Folsom Street, San Francisco, 415/255-1351.

Roaring Mouse Cycles, 1352 Irving Street, San Francisco, 415/753-6272, website: www.roaringmousecycles.com.

Sports Basement, 1301 Sixth Street, San Francisco, 415/437-0100, website: www.sportsbasement.com.

Valencia Cyclery, 1077 Valencia Street, San Francisco, 415/550-6600.

Vision Cyclery S.F., 772 Stanyan Street, San Francisco, 415/221-9766.

San Rafael

Mike's Bicycle Center, 1601 Fourth Street, San Rafael, 415/454-3747, website: www.mikesbicyclecenter.com.

Performance Bike, 369 Third Street, San Rafael, 415/454-9063, website: www.performancebike.com.

Sausalito

A Bicycle Odyssey, 1417 Bridgeway, Sausalito, 415/332-3050, website: www.abicycleodyssey.com.

Sausalito Cyclery, 1 Gate Six Road, Sausalito, 415/332-3200, website: www.mikesbicyclecenter.com.

East Bay

Alameda
Alameda Bicycle, 1522 Park Street, Alameda, 510/522-0070, website:
www.alamedabicycle.com.
Bicycles Alameda, 883 Island Drive, Alameda, 510/865-3400.
Cycle City, 1433 High Street, Alameda, 510/521-2872, website:
www.cyclecityusa.com.
Stone's, 2320 Santa Clara Avenue, Alameda, 510/523-3264.

Albany
Solano Avenue Cyclery, 1554 Solano Avenue, Albany, 510/524-1094, website:
www.solanoavenuecyclery.com.

Antioch
Bikes for Life, 1344 Sunset Drive, Antioch, 925/754-8025.
Schwinn City, 814 A Street, Antioch, 925/757-0664.

Berkeley
Bent Spoke, 1615 University Avenue, Berkeley, 510/540-0583.
Left Coast Cyclery, 2928 Domingo Avenue, Berkeley, 510/204-8550,
website: www.leftcoastcyclery.com.
Mike's Bikes, 2133 University Avenue, Berkeley, 510/549-8350, website:
www.mikesbicyclecenter.com.
Missing Link Bicycle Shop, 1988 Shattuck Avenue, Berkeley,
510/843-7471, website: www.missinglink.org.
REI, 1338 San Pablo Avenue, Berkeley, 510/527-4140, website: www.rei.com.
Velo Sport, 1650 Martin Luther King Way, Berkeley, 510/849-0437.

Brentwood
Brentwood Cyclery, Inc., 3901-A Walnut Boulevard, Brentwood, 925/634-5600.

Castro Valley
Castro Valley Cyclery, 20515 Stanton Avenue, Castro Valley,
510/538-1878, website: www.cvcyclery.com.
Eden Bicycles, 3313 Village Drive, Castro Valley, 510/881-5000, website:
www.edenbicycles.com.

Clayton

Clayton Bicycle Center, 5411 Clayton Road, Clayton, 925/672-2522.

Concord

REI, 1975 Diamond Boulevard, Concord, 925/825-9400, website: www.rei.com.

Danville

California Pedaler, 495 Hartz Avenue, Danville, 925/820-0345, website: www.californiapedaler.com.

Danville Bikes, 115 Hartz Avenue, Danville, 925/837-0966.

Pegasus Bicycle Works, 439 Rail Road Avenue, Danville, 925/362-2220, website: www.pegasusbicycleworks.com.

Alamo Bikes, 1469 Danville Boulevard, Danville, 925/837-8444.

Dublin

Dublin Cyclery, 7001 Dublin Boulevard, Dublin, 925/828-8676, website: www.dublincyclery.com.

El Sobrante

El Sobrante Schwinn Cyclery, 5057 El Portal Drive, El Sobrante, 510/223-3440.

The Pedaler, 3826 San Pablo Dam Road, El Sobrante, 510/222-3420, website: www.theped.com.

Fremont

The Bicycle Garage, 4673 Thornton Avenue, Suite A, Fremont, 510/795-9622.

Performance Bike, 39121 Fremont Boulevard, Fremont, 510/494-1466, website: www.performancebike.com.

REI, 43962 Fremont Boulevard, Fremont, 510/651-0305, website: www.rei.com.

Tri City Sporting Goods, 40900 Grimmer Boulevard, Fremont, 510/651-9600.

Hayward

Cyclepath, 22510 Foothill Boulevard, Hayward, 510/881-5177, website: www.cyclepathhayward.com.

Witt's Bicycle Shop, 22125 Mission Boulevard, Hayward, 510/538-8771.

Lafayette

Hank and Frank Bicycles, 3377 Mt. Diablo Boulevard, Lafayette, 925/376-2453.

Sharp Bicycle, 969 Moraga Road, Lafayette, 925/284-9616.

Livermore

Livermore Cyclery, 2288 First Street, Livermore, 925/455-8090, website: www.livermorecyclery.com.

Cal Bicycles, 2106 First Street, Livermore, 925/447-6666, website: www.calbicycles.com.

Martinez

Martinez Cyclery, 4990 Pacheco Boulevard, Martinez, 925/228-9050, website: www.martinezcyclery.com.

Oakland

A Round World Bike Shop, 2900 Linden Street, Oakland, 510/835-8763.

Cycle Sports, 3241 Grand Avenue, Oakland, 510/444-7900, website: www.cyclesportsonline.com.

Hank and Frank Bicycles, 6030 College Avenue, Oakland, 510/658-1177.

Wheels of Justice, 1969 Mountain Boulevard, Oakland, 510/339-6091, website: www.wojcyclery.com.

Pioneer Bike Shop, 11 Rio Vista Avenue, Oakland, 510/658-8981.

Pleasant Hill

Mike's Bikes, 1741 Contra Costa Boulevard, Pleasant Hill, 925/671-9127, website: www.mikesbicycles.com.

Pleasant Hill Cyclery, 1494 Contra Costa Boulevard, Pleasant Hill, 925/676-2667, website: www.pleasanthillcyclery.com.

Pleasanton

Bicycles Pleasanton, 525 Main Street, Pleasanton, 925/461-0905.

San Leandro

Robinson Wheel Works, 1235 MacArthur Boulevard, San Leandro, 510/352-4663, website: www.robinsonwheelworks.com.

Walnut Creek

Encina Bicycle, 2901 Ygnacio Valley Road, Walnut Creek, 925/944-9200, website: www.encinacycles.com.

Performance Bike, 1401 North Broadway, Walnut Creek, 925/937-7723, website: www.performancebike.com.

Rivendell Bicycle Works, 2040 North Main Street, Walnut Creek, 925/933-7304, website: www.rivendellbicycles.com.

Peninsula and South Bay

Belmont
California Sports & Cyclery, 1464 El Camino Real, Belmont, 650/593-8806.

Burlingame
Summit Bicycles, 1111 Burlingame Avenue, Burlingame, 650/343-8483, website: www.summitbicycles.com.

Campbell
Performance Bike, 1646 South Bascom Avenue, Campbell, 408/559-0495, website: www.performancebike.com.

Wheel Away Cycle Center, 402 East Hamilton Avenue, Campbell, 408/378-4636.

Cupertino
Cupertino Bike Shop, 10493 South De Anza Boulevard, Cupertino, 408/255-2217, website: www.cupertinobike.com.

Daly City
Broadmoor Bicycles, 150 San Pedro Road, Daly City, 650/756-1120, website: www.broadmoorbicycles.com.

Half Moon Bay
The Bike Works, 20 Stone Pine Center, Half Moon Bay, 650/726-6708.

Bicyclery, 101 Main Street, Suite B, Half Moon Bay, 650/726-6000.

Los Altos
The Bicycle Outfitter, 963 Fremont Avenue, Los Altos, 650/948-8092, website: www.bicycleoutfitter.com.

Chain Reaction Bicycles, 2310 Homestead Road, Los Altos, 408/735-8735, website: www.chainreaction.com.

Los Gatos
Crossroads Bicycles, 217 North Santa Cruz Avenue, Los Gatos, 408/354-0555.

Los Gatos Cyclery, 652 North Santa Cruz Avenue, Los Gatos, 408/399-5099, website: www.losgatoscyclery.com.

Summit Bicycles, 111 East Main Street, Los Gatos, 408/399-9142, website: www.summitbicycles.com.

Menlo Park

Menlo Velo, 433 El Camino Real, Menlo Park, 650/327-5137.

The Bike Connection, 622 Santa Cruz Avenue, Menlo Park, 650/327-3318.

Milpitas

Sun Bike Shop, 1549 Landess Avenue, Milpitas, 408/262-4360.

Mountain View

Off Ramp, 2320 El Camino Real, Mountain View, 650/968-2974.

Palo Alto

Bike Connection, 2011 El Camino Real, Palo Alto, 650/424-8034, website: www.bikeconnection.net.

Mike's Bikes, 2180 El Camino Real, Palo Alto, 650/493-8776, website: www.mikes-bicyclecenter.com.

Palo Alto Bicycles, 171 University Avenue, Palo Alto, 650/328-7411, website: www.paloaltobicycles.com.

Redwood City

Chain Reaction Bicycles, 1451 El Camino Real, Redwood City, 650/366-7130, website: www.chainreaction.com.

Go Ride Bicycles, 2755 El Camino Real, Redwood City, 650/366-2453.

Performance Bike, 2535 El Camino Real, Redwood City, 650/365-9094, website: www.performancebike.com.

San Bruno

Bike Route, 568 San Mateo Avenue, San Bruno, 650/873-9555, website: www.bike routeinc.com.

San Carlos

Broken Spoke, 782 Laurel Street, San Carlos, 650/594-9210.

REI, 1119 Industrial Boulevard, San Carlos, 650/508-2330, website: www.rei.com.

Velo Bicycle Shop, 1316 El Camino Real, San Carlos, 650/591-2210.

San Jose

Calabazas Cyclery, 6140 Bollinger Road, San Jose, 408/366-2453, website: www.calabazas.com.

Fast Bicycle, 2274 Alum Rock Avenue, San Jose, 408/251-9110.

The Hyland Family's Bicycles, 1515 Meridian Avenue, San Jose, 408/269-2300, website: www.hylandbikes.com.

Pacific Bicycle, 1008 Blossom Hill Road, San Jose, 408/264-3570, website: www.pacbikeonline.com.

Reed's Sport Shop, 3020 Alum Rock Avenue, San Jose, 408/926-1600, website: www.reedssportshop.com.

REI, 400 El Paseo de Saratoga Shopping Center, San Jose, 408/871-8765, website: www.rei.com.

Santa Teresa Bikes, 503 West Capitol Expressway, San Jose, 408/264-2453, website: www.fifthwave.com/stbikes.

Trail Head Cyclery, 14450 Union Avenue, San Jose, 408/369-9666, website: www.trailheadonline.com.

Willow Glen Bicycles, 1110 Willow Street, San Jose, 408/293-2606, website: www.willowglenbicycles.com.

San Mateo

Cyclepath, 1212 South El Camino Real, San Mateo, 650/341-0922, website: www.cyclepath.com.

Talbots Cyclery, 445 South B Street, San Mateo, 650/342-0184.

Santa Clara

Calmar Cycles, 2236 El Camino Real, Santa Clara, 408/249-6907, website: www.calmarcycles.com.

The Off Ramp, 2369 El Camino Real, Santa Clara, 408/249-2848, website: www.offrampbicycles.com.

Shaws' Lightweight Cycles, 45 Washington Street, Santa Clara, 408/246-7881, website: www.shawscycles.com.

Sunnyvale

Walt's Cycles, 116 Carroll Street, Sunnyvale, 408/736-2630, website: www.waltscycles.com.

INDEX

NOTES

NOTES

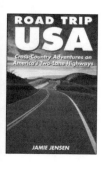